# The Fall of Rome and Constantinople: The History of the Attacks that Destroyed the Western Roman Empire and Byzantine Empire

## By Charles River Editors

**Évariste Vital Luminais'** *The Sack of Rome*

# About Charles River Editors

**Charles River Editors** provides superior editing and original writing services across the digital publishing industry, with the expertise to create digital content for publishers across a vast range of subject matter. In addition to providing original digital content for third party publishers, we also republish civilization's greatest literary works, bringing them to new generations of readers via ebooks.

Sign up here to receive updates about free books as we publish them, and visit Our Kindle Author Page to browse today's free promotions and our most recently published Kindle titles.

# Introduction

**J.N. Sylvestre's painting of the 410 sack of Rome**

"The City which had taken the whole world was itself taken." - St. Jerome

For the people of the ancient Mediterranean and beyond, the city of Rome had been a symbol of power for centuries, and entering the early 5th century CE, the Eternal City hadn't been taken by an enemy force since the Gauls had done it about 800 years, an unheard of period of tranquility in a world wracked with almost constant warfare.

Thus, when the Visigoths, whom the Romans considered uncultured and inferior, took the city of Rome and sacked it in 410, the world was stunned. It made theologians of the newly Christianized empire question God's plan on Earth, and it encouraged many leading Romans to look east to Constantinople for their future. Indeed, the Western Roman Empire would completely collapse in the late 5th century, less than 70 years after the Visigoths sacked Rome, and just how it went from being a superpower to a poorly led, weak, and vulnerable shadow of its former self has preoccupied historians for centuries.

To this day, it remains difficult to trace just when the decline began, but it's fair to say that the sack of Rome was the result of a number of factors that had been coalescing for many years. Only Roman arrogance kept the empire from seeing the grave peril its capital was in, which helped bring about the events leading up to the fall of Rome itself. The Latin phrase *imperium sine fine* ("empire without end") neatly summed up not just the geographic reach of the mighty empire, but the feeling that it would never end. Nonetheless, little more than 300 years after the end of the *Pax Romana*, the Western Roman Empire had all but ceased to exist. During the same period, the population of the city of Rome itself declined from over a million people to less than 30,000. Within the walls of Rome, vast areas returned to pastureland and shepherds grazed their flocks in a surreal landscape where the ruins of structures representing the might of the empire, such as the Patheon, Colosseum and Theatre of Marcellus, rose above a barren vista of scrub and forest.

In the end, the fall of the Roman Empire was not a tale of cataclysmic events that shattered the sprawling power, but the culmination of centuries of internal dissent and decay, combined with growing external threats that led to gradual decline and eventually to the empire's final destruction.

It would be hard if not outright impossible to overstate the impact Constantine I had on the history of Christianity, Rome, and Europe as a whole. Best known as Constantine the Great, the kind of moniker only earned by rulers who distinguished themselves in battle and conquest, Constantine remains an influential and controversial figure to this day. He achieved enduring fame by being the first Roman emperor to personally convert to Christianity, and for the Edict of Milan, the imperial decree which legalized the worship of Christ and promoted religious freedom throughout the Empire. More than 1500 years after Constantine's death, Abdu'l-Bahá, the head of the Bahá'í Faith, wrote, "His blessed name shines out across the dawn of history like the morning star, and his rank and fame among the world's noblest and most highly civilized is still on the tongues of Christians of all denominations"

Moreover, even though he is best remembered for his religious reforms and what his (mostly Christian) admirers described as his spiritual enlightenment, Constantine was also an able and effective ruler in his own right. Rising to power in a period of decline and confusion for the Roman Empire, he gave it a new and unexpected lease on life by repelling the repeated invasions of the Germanic tribes on the Northern and Eastern borders of the Roman domains, even going so far as to re-expand the frontier into parts of Trajan's old conquest of Dacia (modern Romania), which had been abandoned as strategically untenable.

However, it can be argued that despite his military successes – the most notable of which occurred fighting for supremacy against other Romans – Constantine may well have set the stage for the ultimate collapse of the Roman Empire as it had existed up until that point. It was Constantine who first decided that Rome, exposed and vulnerable near the gathering masses of barbarians moving into Germania and Gaul, was a strategically unsafe base for the Empire, and thus expanded the city of New Rome on the Dardanelles straits, creating what eventually became Constantinople. By moving the political, administrative and military capital of the Empire from Rome to the East, as well as the Imperial court with all its attendant followers, Constantine laid the groundwork for the eventual schism which saw the two parts of the Roman Empire become two entirely separate entities, go their own way, and eventually collapse piecemeal under repeated waves of invasion.

In terms of geopolitics, perhaps the most seminal event of the Middle Ages was the successful Ottoman siege of Constantinople in 1453. The city had been an imperial capital as far back as the 4th century, when Constantine the Great shifted the power center of the Roman Empire there, effectively establishing two almost equally powerful halves of antiquity's greatest empire. Constantinople would continue to serve as the capital of the Byzantine Empire even after the Western half of the Roman Empire collapsed in the late 5th century. Naturally, the Ottoman Empire would also use Constantinople as the capital of its empire after their conquest effectively ended the Byzantine Empire, and thanks to its strategic location, it has been a trading center for years and remains one today under the Turkish name of Istanbul.

The end of the Byzantine Empire had a profound effect not only on the Middle East but Europe as well. Constantinople had played a crucial part in the Crusades, and the fall of the Byzantines meant that the Ottomans now shared a border with Europe. The Islamic empire was viewed as a threat by the predominantly Christian continent to their west, and it took little time for different European nations to start clashing with the powerful Turks. In fact, the Ottomans would clash with Russians, Austrians, Venetians, Polish, and more before collapsing as a result of World

War I, when they were part of the Central Powers.

The Ottoman conquest of Constantinople also played a decisive role in fostering the Renaissance in Western Europe. The Byzantine Empire's influence had helped ensure that it was the custodian of various ancient texts, most notably from the ancient Greeks, and when Constantinople fell, Byzantine refugees flocked west to seek refuge in Europe. Those refugees brought books that helped spark an interest in antiquity that fueled the Italian Renaissance and essentially put an end to the Middle Ages altogether.

The Fall of Rome and Constantinople: The History of the Attacks that Destroyed the Western Roman Empire and Byzantine Empire

About Charles River Editors

Introduction

  A Golden Era

  Cracks

  The Crisis of the Third Century

  The Sack of Rome

  The Fall of the Western Roman Empire

  Reunification Efforts

  The Rise of the Ottomans

  The Byzantine Empire Before the Fall of Constantinople

  The Fall of Constantinople

  Online Resources

  Further Reading about the Fall of Rome

  Further Reading about the Fall of Constantinople

# A Golden Era

In 509 BCE, the city-state of Rome established something new and dramatic: rule not by a monarch, but by two consuls who were to be elected for a period of one year and by a Senate, a debating chamber formed by elected senators. This was not a true democratic system as we now understand it: only a very limited number of wealthy people were permitted to vote, for example, and, to become a senatorial candidate, a man (for women were not permitted to participate) had to show personal assets of over one million sesterces. However, this system of government was an attempt to protect the city from the potential excesses of a single ruler. Each consul was expected to act as a check on the power of the other, and any consul or senator who misbehaved while in office could be prosecuted once his term was over.

Under this system of republican rule, Rome prospered and expanded. By 218 BCE, Rome controlled the entire Italian peninsula in addition to the islands of Sicily, Sardinia and Corsica. After a series of successful wars with the powerful African Empire of Carthage, Roman influence expanded over much of southern Spain and the east coast of the Adriatic Sea as far south as Greece. By 20 BCE, Rome controlled almost all of Spain, much of France, the North African coast of the Mediterranean, Greece and a large part of Turkey.

By this time, the apparatus of republican government was firmly in place. The consuls ruled, the Senate debated and passed new laws and the power of the state was enforced by the army. The Roman army was one of the best trained, best equipped and most effective of the period and its power led to a relentless expansion of the borders of the empire. However, the very power of the army proved to be a threat to the republic.

In theory, the Senate had absolute power over the deployment and use of the Roman army, but in fact, military leaders began to assume more and more power. Gaius Marius (157 BCE – 86 BCE) for example, was both a successful military leader and a consul, a position to which he was elected an unprecedented seven times. Marius led the Roman army in successful campaigns against two Germanic tribes - the Cimbri and the Teutones, but he also instituted important changes within the army. In simple terms, as the borders of the republic expanded, the available manpower in the city of Rome was not sufficient to protect Roman interests across a sprawling territory.

Marius reformed the way in which recruitment to the army was done, removing previous requirements that soldiers had to be volunteers who were also property owners. Instead, he allowed volunteers to join the army from the poorest classes in Rome, leading to an influx of the urban poor in the army. This provided the needed boost in numbers, but it also caused a fundamental shift in the composition of the army. Instead of being formed of people who were primarily loyal to the republic, army units, instead, became loyal to their commanders who not only led them in battle, but also paid their wages and became, effectively, patrons for their troops.

Even while Marius was winning plaudits for his military exploits, another Roman General, Lucius Cornelius Sulla, was plotting to overthrow the republic and establish his own dictatorship. After a successful campaign in the east, Sulla returned to Rome with his army. Two military factions, the armies of Marius and Sulla, clashed close to the city. Sulla was victorious and imposed his will on the Senate. Soon, he was forced to leave the city to lead a Roman army against Mithridates in Greece. He was victorious, but when he returned, Marius, who had taken refuge in Africa with his army, had retaken Rome and had many of Sulla's supporters executed.

Marius died of an unknown illness in 86 BCE, leaving Sulla as the undisputed dictator of Rome. However, in 79 BCE, Sulla resigned his dictatorship and retired to his country home before his death in 78 BCE. The Senate and the republic returned to normal, but the issue of military leaders assuming political power and armies that were loyal only to their commanders would prove to be a threat to Rome that was never entirely addressed.

The man who would finally bring about the end of the Roman Republic was Gaius Julius Caesar, a military leader as well as a politician. Caesar was highly intelligent, wildly ambitious and utterly ruthless. After leading a number of successful military campaigns, Caesar entered an alliance with two of the most powerful men in Rome: Gnaeus Pompeius Magnus (Pompey the Great), another general, and Marcus Licinius Crassus, a wealthy politician. The three men formed the First Triumvirate, a political alliance that effectively controlled Rome and the Senate for several years after 60 BCE.

After the death of Crassus in 53 BCE, a confrontation between Caesar and Pompey was all but inevitable. A civil war finally erupted in 45 BCE and Caesar's victory left him as the undisputed leader of Rome. He was elected *dictator perpetuo* (dictator for life) and began to institute sweeping changes that angered the ruling elites to whom he was opposed. This opposition resulted in the assassination of Caesar by a faction of rebellious senators in 44 BCE.

This led directly to another civil war led on one side by Caesar's great-nephew Gaius Octavius (Octavian) supported by two generals and politicians, Marcus Antonius (Mark Antony) and Marcus Aemilius Lepidus. This faction, known as the Second Triumvirate, fought against the assassins of Caesar led by Brutus and Cassius. With victory at the Battle of Phillipi in 42 BCE, the members of the Second Triumvirate took control of Rome. However, disagreements between the three led to further wars that culminated in the exile of Lepidus in 36 BCE and the defeat of Marcus Antonius by Octavian at the Battle of Actium in 31 BCE.

Initially, Octavian made a show of returning power to the Senate. However, he retained his military power and gradually instituted a series of changes that led to his accession to total power. By 27 BCE, the Senate had granted Octavian two titles: *Augustus* (the illustrious one) and *Princeps* (First Citizen). Although the title "Emperor" had not yet been formally used, most historians cite 27 BCE as the year that marked the end of the Roman Republic and the beginning of the Roman Empire.

By the time of Augustus's death in 14 CE, the territory under direct Roman control had expanded exponentially. On his deathbed, Augustus was claimed to have said, "*Marmoream se relinquere, quam latericiam accepisset*"[1] ("Behold, I found Rome of clay, and leave her to you of marble"). Roman troops controlled Hispania (modern-day Spain and Portugal), Raetia and Noricum (modern-day Switzerland, Bavaria, Austria, and Slovenia), and Illyricum and Pannonia (modern-day Albania, Croatia, Hungary and Serbia).

---

[1] Eck, Werner; Takács, Sarolta A., *The Age of Augustus*, translated by Deborah Lucas Schneider, Oxford: Blackwell Publishing, 2003.

Galatia (modern-day Turkey) became a Roman province in 25 BCE, and Roman holdings in North Africa and modern-day Syria expanded notably. Rome had become the center of an empire larger than any other in the west and the position of emperor established by Augustus became central to the continuation of that empire.

Although the Senate still existed, the Roman emperor effectively had absolute power over all the people within the empire. The name Caesar became synonymous with the role of emperor: the terms Kaiser, used for the ruler of Germany, and Tzar, the ruler of Russia, both derive from Caesar.

However, Augustus also established an even more significant precedent: that the Roman Emperor would choose his successor. This was done to ensure that the role of emperor would continue and that an unbroken line of emperors would rule Rome. However, while this guaranteed stability and seemed to be a way of avoiding civil wars arising from competing claims for the role, it also ensured that the emperor himself would be the defining factor in the rule of the empire. While the emperor was someone capable and focused on the good of the empire such as Augustus, this worked well. However, if the emperor was weak, selfish or unstable, this would have negative implications for the welfare of Rome. Within this system instituted by Augustus were sown the seeds that would eventually lead to the downfall of the empire itself.

Augustus' immediate successor was his step-son, Tiberius Caesar Augustus. Tiberius was reluctant to become emperor though he quickly proved to be an efficient administrator. However, his distaste for public life and the formal duties of the emperor led to his becoming more reclusive until, in 26 CE, after 12 years of rule, he withdrew to the island of Capri in the Bay of Naples, leaving Rome effectively under the control of the leader of the Praetorian Guard, Lucius Aelius Sejanus.

Sejanus quickly moved the guard from their traditional encampments outside the city into quarters in the heart of Rome. With more than 9,000 loyal troops at his disposal, Sejanus began a brutal campaign of repression against opponents of Tiberius. Sejanus also began building his own power base within the city and he clearly saw himself as a potential successor to Tiberius.

However, Sejanus' brutality encouraged opposition that eventually persuaded the emperor to act: Sejanus and many of his supporters were executed or exiled in 31 CE. Tiberius continued to rule from Capri until his death at the age of 77 in 37 CE.

As his successor, he named his nephew, Gaius Caesar Augustus Germanicus, popularly known as Caligula (Little Boots). The Emperor Caligula would rule for just four years, but his brief period in power graphically demonstrated the flaws in the system of rule by the emperor. Caligula was not just vain, unpredictable and selfish, he was almost certainly also insane. He began appearing in public dressed as various gods, including Hercules, Mercury, Venus and Apollo. He insisted that he be addressed as a god and, on one occasion, led a Roman army in battle against a fellow-god who he claimed was not showing sufficient respect: Neptune, god of the sea. Caligula had his men slash at the waves with their swords and then returned to Rome in triumph bearing "booty" from the war (sea shells collected by his troops).

He was said to have had had people killed on a whim and occasionally because he was bored. On one occasion, it is claimed that while attending games in Rome, he became irritated when he discovered that no prisoners were available to be killed during the interval. He then had members of the Praetorian Guard toss members of the audience into the ring where they were devoured by wild animals.[2] Caligula also squandered a great deal of the empire's wealth on personal projects and, in 40 CE, announced that he was planning to relocate permanently to Egypt where he expected to be worshipped as a living god. Caligula was assassinated in 41 CE by a group of enraged senators. They had hoped that they would be able to use this event to restore the republic, but a faction of the Praetorian Guard instead seized Caligula's uncle Claudius who they acclaimed as the next Emperor of Rome. Faced with this fait-accompli, the Senate was forced to agree.

Claudius proved to be a conscientious and intelligent emperor who continued the expansion of the empire (including an occupation of Britain) and restored the depleted treasury. However, Caligula's brief reign was a graphic warning that the system of rule by the emperor brought its own particular hazards.

---

[2] Gregory S. Aldrete, *Daily Life in the Roman City: Rome, Pompeii, and Ostia*, Greenwood, 2004.

By 96 CE, a group of emperors from a different Roman family, the Nervan-Antonin Dynasty, came to power. Five of these emperors - Nerva, Trajan, Hadrian, Antoninus Pius, and Marcus Aurelius, proved to be effective and capable (they became known in Rome as the "Five Good Emperors"). It was said of this period, "The Roman Empire was governed by absolute power, under the guidance of wisdom and virtue."[3]

During their reigns, the empire grew to its largest extent. By 117 CE, the Roman Empire (and territory controlled by its allies) covered an area of more than 2 million square miles and encompassed a population of over 120 million people (though only a fraction of these were Roman citizens).

By that point, the Roman permanent army had grown to 150,000 men supported by a similar number of "auxiliaries," friendly troops from other states. The movement of this army to all parts of the empire was facilitated by a network of roads more comprehensive than any previously seen. However, there were no remaining significant rival empires for the Roman army to fight, and most conflict during this period was

---
[3] Edward Gibbon, *The History of the Decline and Fall of the Roman Empire,* London, 1776.

restricted to battles with "barbarians," people who lived outside the empire and were unaffected by its laws, culture or society.

Most citizens of the empire had access to ample food and production capacity, trade volume and resource extraction were efficient and was supported by an effective transport infrastructure: "An interchange of goods between the various provinces rapidly developed, which soon reached a scale unprecedented in previous history and not repeated until a few centuries ago."[4]

The phrase imperium sine fine (empire without end) became not a boast, but a simple statement of fact. For most people, it was difficult to envisage a world that was <u>not</u> dominated by the city of Rome. However, even though it was not readily apparent at the time, Rome was reaching the end of it greatest period of expansion and consolidation.

## Cracks

The beginning of the end of what would retrospectively have been seen as the greatest period of the Roman Empire began with the death of the last of

---

[4] Henry St. Lawrence Beaufort Moss, *The Birth of the Middle Ages*, London, 1935.

the Five Good Emperors, Marcus Aurelius, in 180 CE. He was succeeded by his son, the 18-year-old Commodus. Although this new emperor would face few external military threats during his reign, he would struggle with almost constant internal intrigue and plots.

**Eric Gaba's picture of a bust of Marcus Aurelius**

## A bust depicting Commodus as Hercules

In 182 CE, after less than two years as emperor, there was an assassination attempt on Commodus as he entered a theatre in Rome. The two assassins were seized by the emperor's guards and rapidly confessed that they had been sent to kill Commodus as part of a conspiracy engineered by his eldest sister, Lucilla. The assassins were executed and Lucilla was exiled and later killed. Disheartened by this attempt on his life,

Commodus spent less and less time in the city of Rome, preferring instead to live on the family estates at Lanuvium. To rule in his absence, Commodus appointed a new chamberlain, Cleander, a Phrygian freedman who was married to one of the emperor's mistresses, Demostratia.

Cleander used this opportunity to enrich himself. He began selling public offices, military leaderships and even membership of the Senate to the highest bidder. As a direct result, unrest within the empire and particularly within the army, increased. Deserters from the army began to cause problems in Gaul and Germania. In 187 CE, one of the leaders of the deserters, Maternus, traveled to Rome from Gaul intending to assassinate Commodus who was scheduled to make one of his rare public appearances in Rome at the Festival of the Great Goddess. The plot was uncovered and Maternus was executed before he could reach the emperor but, convinced that his life was at risk, the emperor again retreated to his family home.

In the spring of 190 CE, Rome suffered a food shortage that brought the prospect of starvation to many people in the city for the first time in living memory.

During a race at the Circus Maximus, a mob began demonstrating against Cleander who they blamed for the lack of food. Cleander was forced to flee to Commodus' estate at Lanuvium, but he was pursued by members of the mob who loudly demanded his head. Commodus, terrified, had Cleander beheaded, and this was followed by a spate of executions of Cleander's supporters.

The following year, a fire ravaged many parts of the city of Rome, destroying important buildings and large numbers of ordinary houses. Commodus' response infuriated many Roman citizens and seemed to reinforce claims that he was descending into megalomania. He announced that the city would be rebuilt after the fire, but that henceforth it would be called Colonia Lucia Annia Commodiana (the city of Commodus) and that the Senate was to be rebranded as the Commodian Fortunate Senate. Even the months of the year were to be renamed: Commodus had given himself twelve names and from now on, the months of the year would bear these names.[5]

Commodus had always been interested in sport and

---
[5] Dio Cassius, *Roman History*, English translation by Loeb Classical Library, 1927.

fitness and believed himself to be a capable fighter. He had slaves sent to his estate at Lanuvium to act as sparring partners while he practiced his skills as a gladiator. This was not a popular assignment as Commodus always killed these unwilling partners. Then, he announced that he would fight as a gladiator in the arena in Rome. Clearly, it wouldn't do if the emperor was to lose, so his opponents were always carefully chosen: a few were disabled veterans with missing limbs and at least one was a dwarf. Commodus charged the city treasury for the honor of having him take part, demanding an eye-watering one million sesterces for each combat in which he participated. Soon, the city was running perilously short of funds.

Commodus' end came when he announced towards the end of 192 CE that he would begin 193 by continuing his ruinously expensive gladiatorial career, as well as instituting some new changes in the city. He also drew up a list of people he intended to have executed to celebrate the New Year. One of those people was his long-term mistress, Marcia. She found the list and saw her name on it. It also contained the names of several others marked for death including the prefects Laetus and Eclectus. Marcia showed the list to the other two and all three agreed that they must kill the emperor before he could carry out these executions. On 31st December 192 CE, Marcia put poison in Commodus' food. It had little effect beyond causing the emperor to vomit. While recovering in the bath, Commodus was strangled by Narcissus, one of his gladiatorial trainers.

Upon his death, the Senate named Commodus as *de facto damnatio memoriae* (a public enemy) and announced that the city of Rome (and all the other institutions renamed by Commodus) would revert to their original names. The reign of Commodus was marked not by external pressure on the empire, but by internal plots that helped to destabilize it.

The year that followed proved to be even worse. Commodus' immediate successor was the proconsul of Africa, Publius Helvius Pertinax. His rule lasted less than 90 days and culminated in his murder by members of the Praetorian Guard. The guard then auctioned the position of emperor to the highest bidder. Marcus Didius Julianus came out on top by promising each member of the Guard 25,000 sesterces in return for their support. He became emperor in early April 193.

However, the governors of three Roman provinces - Syria, Britain, and Pannonia Superior, announced they would not support this new appointment and two of them, Septimius Severus and Gaius Pescennius Niger, sent armies marching towards Rome. Panicked, the Senate confirmed the appointment of Septimius Severus as the new emperor and Didius Julianus was quietly murdered in the palace on 1st June, just 60 days after becoming emperor.

Septimius Severus arrived in Rome with his army and was immediately declared emperor. However, even as this was happening, the Roman governor of Britain and Spain, Decimus Clodius Albinus, was declared to be the new emperor by his troops. Meanwhile, Gaius Pescennius Niger claimed that he was really the Emperor of Rome and continued to advance on the city.

**Sailko's picture of a bust of Clodius**

Little wonder the year 193 CE was known thereafter as the "Year of the Five Emperors." Unable to fight both rival claimants at the same time, Septimius Severus formed an alliance with Decimus Clodius Albinus while fighting an all-out war with the forces under the command of Gaius Pescennius Niger. Niger's army was finally defeated (and Niger killed) in 194 CE. Back in Rome, Decimus Clodius Albinus was becoming uneasy: he had assumed that he would take on the role of emperor in the event of the death of Septimius Severus and was incensed when, instead, the emperor announced that his son would be his successor. Albinus returned to the provinces where, in 197 CE, he once again declared himself emperor. After a series of bloody battles, Albinus was finally defeated and killed at the Battle of Lugdunum in February 197 CE. After four years of internecine warfare had weakened the empire, Septimius Severus finally became the undisputed Emperor of Rome.

The "Year of the Five Emperors" graphically illustrated one of the main weaknesses inherent in the Roman Empire: the uncertain process involved in the selection of a successor to the existing emperor. There were no clear rules for choosing a successor: there was no system of hereditary succession as seen in other empires and states, though a family connection to the previous emperor was often beneficial to claimants. Although the empire was essentially a dictatorship under the control of the emperor, Rome also retained many of the trappings of the previous republic, including the Senate.

Thus, the opinion of senators had to be taken into

account when choosing a new emperor. The army also had a role in choosing the new ruler, particularly the men of the Praetorian Guard. Any claimant who lacked the support of the army was unlikely to succeed, or at least unlikely to stay in power long. Thus, any military commander with a sizeable army behind him might be tempted to put forward his own claim to be the next emperor.

This confused, confusing and muddled system of succession caused internal strife and even long-term civil war that would weaken the empire.

Septimius Severus was clearly aware of these issues and was very careful to ensure that he knew precisely who would succeed him when he died, founding the Severan Dynasty. Unfortunately, this simply confirmed the other major flaw in the system: if the emperor was less than capable, he could undermine the whole mechanism of the empire.

**A bust of Septimius Severus**

Unsurprisingly, one of the first actions that Septimius Severus took on assuming the role of emperor was to dismiss all serving members of the Praetorian Guard. The men who had murdered Pertinax and auctioned off the role of emperor were banished from Rome and forbidden to come within 100 miles of the city, on pain of death. However, the new emperor then promptly formed ten new cohorts of the guard with men drawn exclusively from his own loyal legions.

He also purged the Senate. Large numbers of senators were summarily executed on charges of conspiracy, and these men were quickly replaced with senators loyal to the new emperor. With his base in Rome secure, Severus set about expanding the borders of the empire. First, he led armies in Africa and, during 203/204 CE, conquered new territory in Numidia and fortified existing Roman bases in the region. In 208 CE, he turned his attention to Britain.

The first Roman invasion of Britain had been led by Julius Caesar and subsequent emperors had secured and increased Roman holdings in modern-day England and Wales. However, in Caledonia in the north (present-day Scotland), the Roman occupation was far less successful. In general, Roman control barely extended beyond Hadrian's Wall in the north of England, and Severus was determined to change that. He arrived in England with an army of over 40,000 men and initially made good progress into Caledonia. However, in early 211 CE, Severus fell ill and died in Britain. Once again, the question of imperial succession was to lead to internal dispute and further weakening of the empire.

Severus believed that he had secured the succession by naming his two sons, Lucius Septimius Bassianus and Publius Septimius Geta as co-emperors. It quickly became clear that this was not a viable approach. The Imperial Palace in Rome was divided into two separate areas, one for each emperor, and the two met only occasionally and in the presence of a military guard to forestall any assassination attempt. What little communication that took place happened mainly at the urging of their mother, Julia Domina. By the end of 211 CE, the situation was so difficult that there was talk of splitting the empire into two separate halves, one ruled over by each emperor.

To avoid this, Bassianus (the elder brother) persuaded his mother to arrange a peace meeting in her apartments where the two could talk freely in the absence of guards or advisors. Geta agreed, and when he arrived, was promptly murdered by soldiers smuggled into the meeting area by his brother.

Having a single emperor in charge should have made things better for the empire, but Bassianus proved to be tyrannical, cruel and frankly disinterested in the mundane work of running the empire. Generally known as Caracalla, due to his habit of wearing a hooded cloak, even while sleeping, the emperor was content to leave the day-to-day operation of the empire to his mother while he focused on perceived internal threats to his reign. He gave lavish gifts to the men of the Praetorian Guard in order to assure their loyalty and used these cohorts to assassinate anyone he saw as a threat.

He also proved to have an inordinate liking for massacres during wars, something that decreased the trust of allies and increased resistance in enemies. During a brief foray into Germania, Caracalla is said to have ordered the massacre of an allied military unit simply because he didn't trust their leader. During a visit to Alexandria, Caracalla became incensed when he heard that the locals were making snide jokes about the murder of Geta. In response, the emperor had a number of the population executed. Caracalla's violent reign lasted only until 217 CE when he was assassinated by members of the Praetorian Guard.

The prefect of the Praetorian Guard, Marcus Opelius Macrinus, was suspected of organizing the assassination of Caracalla and this suspicion increased when, a few days later, Macrinus announced that he was now emperor. One of the few significant decisions he made during his brief period of rule was to make peace with the Parthian Empire based in modern-day Iran. This empire, though much smaller than the Roman, had been a source of irritation for some time: Caracalla was on his way to make war on the Parthians when he was assassinated. However, Macrinus also refused to pay the bribes and awards promised by Caracalla to troops in the east. Some, in particular the Gallic Third Legion, entered a state of semi-mutiny as a result, refusing to obey the orders of the new emperor.

At the urging of Julia Domina (and the payment of substantial bribes), the rebellious legions were persuaded to announce their support for Varius Avitus Bassianus, known as Elagabalus, a grandson of Julia Maesa, the sister-in-law of Septimius Severus. Macrinus took his army to Antioch where they faced the supporters of Elagabalus. Macrinus was defeated and killed after just sixteen months as emperor and the victorious troops announced that Elagabalus was now the emperor.

Once established as emperor, the behavior of

Elagabalus soon began to rival that of Caligula, outraging many Romans. He began to refer to himself as a woman and insisted that he be called "Empress," he married his male lover (who was formally installed as the Husband of the Empress) and caused indignation when he insisted also on marrying one of the Vestal Virgins.[6] Realizing that his behavior was likely to lead to rebellion, his grandmother, Julia Maesa, intervened and persuaded the emperor to name a cousin, Severus Alexander, as his successor.

---

[6] Dio Cassius, *Roman History*, English translation by Loeb Classical Library, 1927.

**José Luiz Bernardes Ribeiro's picture of a bust of Elagabalus**

Alexander was popular, especially with the Roman army who found Elagabalus' increasingly bizarre behavior hard to accept. Jealous of this popularity, Elagabalus announced that he had changed his mind and that Severus Alexander was no longer his successor. Enraged members of the Praetorian Guard promptly murdered Elagabalus, his mother and several of his closest advisors. The members of the guard then announced that Severus Alexander was the new emperor.

Severus Alexander became emperor in 222 CE. In a period of just eleven years following the death of Septimius Severus, there had been no fewer than four emperors, all of whom had been killed or assassinated after short periods in office. No empire, no matter how mighty, can continue with the turmoil that such changes inevitably bring. Instead of being focused on protecting the borders of the empire, large military forces were used instead to support one or another of the factions that were trying to put an emperor on the throne.

This also led to a fundamental change in the nature of Roman cities. Instead of relying on the protection of the Roman army, which was often involved in factional fighting during this period, cities increasingly became self-contained, walled communities, capable of protecting themselves if necessary. This, in turn, lessened their reliance on protection provided from Rome and began a process of reducing the power and prestige of that city.

Severus Alexander was just 14-years-old when he became emperor and during the early part of his reign, the day-to-day running of the empire was undertaken by his mother, Julia Avita Mamaea. The new emperor was able to cling to power longer than his predecessors, but he too was killed by his own troops during an unsuccessful campaign in Germania in 235 CE. His death triggered another period of instability and rapid change that would mark the true beginning of the fall of the Roman Empire.

## The Crisis of the Third Century

The 50 years following the assassination of Severus Alexander were some of the most tumultuous ever faced by the Roman Empire. Emperors came and went at a bewildering pace. Many were inept or so focused on protecting their own positions that they had little time to think about the external threats facing the empire. There was still no other empire large and powerful enough to directly challenge Rome, but the Sassanid Empire (which had defeated the Parthians) presented a worrying threat on the empire's eastern border. Large confederations of barbarian tribes made a series of attacks into Roman territory in Germania and

Dacia. With a series of emperors entirely focused on protecting their own position, there was little time to think about how to protect the borders of the empire from these growing threats.

It wasn't just enemies that caused problems for the Roman Empire during this period. The Antonine Plague (the first known global pandemic) had caused large numbers of deaths in the late 2nd century, and this was followed by the even more destructive Plague of Cyprian (249 – 262 CE). This second pandemic killed even more people within the empire (some major cities such as Alexandria lost more than 60% of their populations).[7] This led to a shortage of troops for the army and a shortage of people to work on the land. That, in turn, led to food scarcity and even to famine.

The situation was made even worse by hyperinflation that undermined the value of Roman coinage. Septimius Severus raised the base pay of Roman soldiers to almost double its previous level and increased the overall size of the army by more than 25%. None of the short-lived emperors who followed dared to change this, fearing that they might lose the support of the

---

[7] Harper, Kyle, *Pandemics and Passages to Late Antiquity: Rethinking the Plague of c. 249-70 described by Cyprian*, Journal of Roman Archaeology, 2015.

army. Instead, they debased the coinage, using copper and bronze in the manufacture of coins that were supposed to be gold and silver. In 161 CE, the purity of the main Roman coin, the silver denarius, was around 75%. By 265 CE, that purity had fallen to around 0.5% with each coin being made primarily of bronze with only a thin surface coating of silver.[8] The outcome was rampant inflation, uncontrolled price rises of up to 1,000% and a Roman coinage that became virtually worthless.

This hyperinflation had at least one notable side-effect: even more severe food shortages in Roman cities. Traditionally, farmers within the empire had sent their produce over long distances using the extensive road system. The food that they produced would then be sold at markets in major cities. With the devaluation in the currency, there was no longer any incentive to do this. Instead, farmers began to aim for self-sufficiency: growing as much food as possible to feed their own families and workers and using local barter to obtain anything they could not grow. In many large Roman cities, food became increasingly scarce. Facing so many

---

[8] *Hyperinflation in the Roman Empire and its Influence on the Collapse of Rome,* Insider Economy, https://medium.com/insider-economy/hyperinflation-in-the-roman-empire-and-its-influence-on-romes-collapse-446486dcda63.

critical problems, what Rome needed more than anything was stable, capable leadership. What it got instead were twenty-six different claimants to the role of emperor in a period of less than fifty years. This was the Crisis of the Third Century.

On learning of the death of Severus Alexander in 235 CE, the men of the 4th Legion based in Pannonia (incorporating parts of present-day Hungary, Croatia and Austria) announced that their commander, Gaius Julius Verus Maximinus, was the new Emperor of Rome. This military leader was generally known as "Thrax" (the Thracian) and not only was he born far from Rome; he was the first commoner to become emperor. He was supported by the Praetorian Guard, who approved of his stern demeanor and military prowess, but he was bitterly opposed by some members of the Senate who were deeply offended by the notion of Rome being ruled by a man they regarded as little better than a peasant.

Given his military background, it is not surprising that instead of spending time in Rome, Maximinus instead spent the early part of his rule leading Roman armies against barbarian invaders. He led two successful campaigns against German tribes before turning on the Dacians and the Sarmatians in 237 CE. Although these military expeditions were successful, Maximinus' absence from Rome (he would never visit the city during his time as emperor) gave the members of the Senate time and opportunity to plot against him.

In early 238 CE, a rebellious group of farmers and landowners in the Roman province of Africa killed local tax collectors and announced that the governor of that province, the elderly Marcus Antonius Gordianus Sempronianus (known as Gordian I) and his only son, also Marcus Antonius Gordianus Sempronianus (known as Gordian II), were the new co-emperors of Rome. The Senate quickly threw its support behind the new emperors. This proved to be more than a little hasty when, less than three weeks after the announcement, Gordian II was killed fighting a Roman legion in Africa that was loyal to Maximinus and, on hearing news of this, Gordian I promptly killed himself.

This left the Senate in a precarious position. They had announced their support for Gordian I and II and they knew that Maximinus was likely to leave Pannonia and march towards Rome to re-establish his authority. The

Senate quickly elected two of its wealthiest members, Pupienus and Balbinus, to become co-emperors. This enraged many of the ordinary people of Rome who were suffering from the effects of food shortages and hyperinflation. They did not want to be ruled by wealthy patricians and, instead, a large faction supported the young son of Gordian II, Marcus Antonius Gordianus (known as Gordian III).

There were riots on the streets of Rome and instances of running street fights between members of the rival factions. Eventually, the Senate was forced to back down and support Gordian III as the next emperor. The issue of succession became pressing in May 238 CE. Maximinus, leading his army towards Rome, was unexpectedly halted by resistance at the northern Roman city of Aquileia. His army was forced to lay siege to the city, and when this failed to prompt a surrender, his own men killed Maximus, his son and his military and political advisors. His head was mounted on a spear and sent to Rome.

The Senate reacted by retracting their support for Gordian III and announcing that Pupienus and Balbinus were now co-emperors. The people of Rome responded with widespread rioting and civil unrest which led to fires that destroyed large parts of the city. After less than three months as rulers, Pupienus and Balbinus were tortured and murdered by the Praetorian Guard and the Senate announced that the 13-year-old Gordian III was to be the new emperor.

The duties of the emperor were clearly beyond such a young man and his role was largely usurped by members of the Senate and the prefect of the Praetorian Guard, Timesitheus. A resurgence of the threat from the Sassanid Empire in 243 CE led to a Roman army being dispatched to the East. The army was nominally led by the now 18-year-old emperor supported by Timesitheus. At the Battle of Resaena, the Sassanids were driven back and Gordian III briefly returned to Rome in triumph. However, during the campaign, Timesitheus died in unknown circumstances and a new prefect of the Praetorian Guard was appointed: Marcus Julius Philippus Arabs, a Roman citizen born in present-day Syria and generally known as Philip the Arab.

The following year, 244 CE, the Sassanids once again threatened the eastern borders of the empire and

Gordian III again led a Roman army to stop them. This time, he was not successful and in February, Gordian III was killed. Some accounts suggest that he died in battle with the Sassanids, while others suggest an assassination was organized by the prefect of the Praetorian Guard, Philip the Arab. The latter version gained some support when Philip immediately announced that he would be the next emperor.

This was confirmed by the Senate, and Philip quickly negotiated peace with the Sassanids before returning to Rome. He began a massive building program in his home town of Shahba, 90km east of Damascus in Syria: the town was re-named Philippopolis in his honor. However, the massive costs of this project, plus the cost of paying the usual bonus to the army on the accension of a new emperor, left the treasury of Rome seriously short of money. As a result, Philip raised taxes which put even more pressure on a people already suffering from food shortages and the effects of inflation.

From 245 – 248 CE, Philip was engaged in leading Roman armies against a series of incursions in Germania, Dacia and the Balkans, as well as renewed activity by the Sassanids. He was broadly successful in these campaigns and returned to the city of Rome in 248 CE in time to lead its citizens in a celebration marking the city's 1,000th anniversary. These games were a fantastic spectacle, but they simply added to the financial burden on Rome. In order to save money, Philip stopped paying the bribes to Germanic tribes east of the Rhine that had persuaded them not to attack Rome. With no financial incentive to maintain the peace, several of these tribes moved into Roman territory.

In late 238 CE, the Quadi tribes and others attacked Pannonia, the Goths crossed the Danube to attack the Roman province of Moesia and the Carpi mounted a number of incursions into Dacia. The Roman legions in the area reacted by announcing that they had appointed their general, Tiberius Claudius Pacatianus, as emperor. The Senate decided to support Philip, and a military force under the command of Senator Gaius Messius Quintus Decius was sent to Pannonia to quell the uprising and to prevent the further incursion of Germanic tribes into Roman territory.

Decius was successful in quelling the rebellion, but the troops in Pannonia were so impressed by the Senator that they declared him emperor instead. Decius then marched towards Rome and defeated an army led by Philip at Verona in September 249 CE. Philip was either killed during the battle or afterwards by his own troops and Decius was confirmed as the Emperor Trajan Decius in October 249. His reign lasted less than two years, until he was killed fighting the Goths in June 251 CE.

The succession of short-lived emperors continued. After the death of Trajan Decius, few Roman emperors stayed in office for more than two years and many lasted considerably less than that. By 270 CE, instability caused by these changes, continuing food shortages and inflation, had led to the once mighty Roman Empire being reduced to three separate parts: the Gallic Empire included Gaul and Britain, the Palmyrene Empire included former Roman territories in the eastern Mediterranean, while the Roman Empire maintained control over the Italian peninsula and most of central Europe.

It seemed that the Roman Empire was destined to disintegrate. Its only hope was an emperor strong and capable enough to reunite the whole splintering edifice.

Given the rapid succession of short-lived and not particularly effective emperors during the third century, that seemed unlikely, but salvation was soon to appear in the form of a young man from a humble background.

Lucius Domitius Aurelianus was born in 214 CE to a relatively ordinary Roman family who lived near the Danube River. He joined the Roman army in 235 CE and quickly proved himself to be an adept and capable soldier. By the time of the rule of the Emperor Gallienus (260 – 268 CE), he had risen through the ranks to become the commander of all Roman cavalry.

In 268 CE, he participated in a campaign led by the emperor to quell forces loyal to a new claimant to the Imperial throne, a general named Aureolus. During a siege of the northern Italian city of Mediolanum, Gallienus was assassinated and another general, Marcus Aurelius Claudius, was acclaimed as emperor by his troops. During the brief reign of Claudius II, Aurelianus was further promoted to the rank of Magister equitum, effectively making the head of the whole Roman army. Under his leadership and through his astute use of cavalry forces, the Romans won a number of notable victories over the Goths and other German tribes. Then,

Claudius II fell ill, possibly afflicted by the Plague of Cyprian then sweeping though Roman territory. In August 270 CE, he died, and his brother, Marcus Aurelius Claudius Quintillus, took the role of emperor with the support of the Senate. However, the legions serving on the German frontier disapproved of this choice and instead acclaimed their own general, Aurelianus, as emperor. The two claimants faced each other in battle near the ancient northern Roman city of Aquileia. Quintillus was either killed, or committed suicide, and Aurelianus was recognized as the new emperor by the Senate later in 270 CE.

   Almost as soon as he took power, Aurelian began a series of military campaigns that would not only defeat the Empire's barbarian enemies, but would also reunite the shattered empire. Within 12 months of becoming emperor, Aurelian defeated several important German tribes including the Goths, Vandals, Alamanni, Juthungi, and the Sarmatians and drove them all back and out of Roman territory. In 272 CE, he turned his attention to the Palmyrene Empire, the former eastern provinces of the Roman Empire that had declared independence and were then ruled by Queen Zenobia in the city of Palmyra. In a series of brilliant campaigns,

Aurelian defeated the forces of Queen Zenobia and brought all of the eastern provinces back under the direct control of the Roman Empire.

In 274 CE, the emperor turned his attention to the Gallic Empire. Through a combination of diplomacy and the threat of military power, Britain and Gaul quickly agreed to return to the Roman Empire. In just four years, Aurelian had defeated the Germanic tribes that threatened the empire's northern frontier and reunited the three separate parts of the empire back into a single political and military entity.

In 275 CE, he turned towards Persia, determined to end once and for all the threat posed to the Roman Empire by the Sassanid Empire. However, instead of achieving another victory, Aurelian was murdered by a member of the Praetorian Guard who was (wrongly) convinced that he was marked for execution. The stunning achievements of Aurelian in less than five years of rule were a reminder of just what the Roman Empire was capable of under the control of a capable leader. However, it would be almost ten years before another effective and determined emperor would assume control and finish the work of rebuilding and reunification that Aurelian had begun.

Gaius Aurelius Valerius Diocletianus was born somewhere around 244 CE as the son of a humble freedman in the Roman province of Dalmatia. We know little of his early life, but it seems that he served in the Roman army and was promoted, possibly by Aurelian himself. In 282 CE, the Emperor Carus (282 – 283 CE) promoted Diocletianus to the important post of commander of the Protectores domestici, an elite cavalry unit attached to the royal household. Carus died in somewhat mysterious circumstances while leading a Roman army in Persia: some accounts claim he was killed by Persian troops while others maintain that he was struck by lightning. On his death his two sons, Numerian and Carinus, became co-emperors in early 284 CE. However, later the same year, Numerian died in Syria, possibly assassinated.

The Roman army of the east responded by proclaiming Diocletianus as the new emperor. In 285, the armies of Carinus and Diocletianus met near the location of the modern-day city of Belgrade in Serbia. Diocletianus was victorious and Carinus was killed, probably by his own men. Following this victory, both the eastern and western armies acclaimed Diocletianus as emperor. Left with little option, the Senate agreed. Diocletian would rule for almost 20 years and would prove to be a highly effective leader, though he instituted changes that would mark a significant departure for the empire.

Diocletian seemed to have little interest in the city of Rome itself and little respect for the Senate. He did not go to Rome at all after being crowned emperor, choosing instead to lead his armies in a successful campaign against the still troublesome German tribes. During the remainder of his reign, he would personally lead several other successful campaigns against the Sassanid Empire and in quelling a rebellion in Egypt. Overall, he was successful in crushing all actual and potential enemies of the empire.

However, while his military achievements were impressive, he also instituted sweeping changes to the way in which the empire was administered. Local provinces were given more power and autonomy and several important new regional centers were established. He also attempted to halt rampant inflation by introducing price controls and a new coin, the argenteus, with one of the new coins being worth 50 of the old denarius. These changes helped slow inflation, but never completely stopped it: it has been estimated that inflation in the Roman Empire reached a high of 15,000% between 200 and 300 CE[9].

In 285 CE, Diocletian appointed another army officer, Marcus Aurelius Valerius Maximianus, as co-emperor. Although it was not initially formally recognized, Diocletian would effectively become emperor of the eastern provinces, while Maximian would control the western provinces. This was the first step towards what would become a final split between the eastern and western parts of the Roman Empire.

In 293 CE, Diocletian introduced another division of power with the Tetrarchy, a system whereby the two senior emperors, the augusti, ruled with the support of two junior rulers, the caesares. Each of these rulers had responsibility for a particular geographic area of the empire and, notably, none were based in the city of Rome. Instead, the empire was ruled from four tetrarchic capitals at Nicomedia (in present-day Turkey), Sirmium (in present-day Serbia), Mediolanum

---

[9] *Hyperinflation in the Roman Empire and its Influence on the Collapse of Rome,* Insider Economy, https://medium.com/insider-economy/hyperinflation-in-the-roman-empire-and-its-influence-on-romes-collapse-446486dcda63.

(present-day Milan), and Augusta Treverorum (in present-day Germany).

These divisions of power made a great deal of sense in terms of administering a huge and sprawling empire. The Roman Empire had become so large and spread over such a vast expanse of territory that it was beyond the capacity of any single emperor to rule effectively. However, these changes made the city of Rome notably less important within the empire and led to a lessening of the "Roman" character of the empire. It is ironic that Diocletian, while responsible for the reunification of the Roman Empire was also the man who changed its character and made the later split between east and west not just possible, but virtually certain.

## The Sack of Rome

In this time of increasing uncertainty, the Roman people turned to new gods, and while some joined mystery religions such as those that worshipped Mithras, Cybele, and Hermes Trimegistos, others joined the persecuted and secretive faith of Christianity. Over time, both the Christians and the mystery religions gained in popularity, but while Christianity was illegal, it grew enough that many noble families joined the ranks, which ensured churches became more and more visible. Periodic persecutions did little to stop the rise of the new religion, and a major change came with the tolerant and strong reign of Constantine the Great, who ruled jointly or opposed from 306-324 and unopposed from 324-337. In 313, Constantine ended the persecution of the Christians with the Edict of Milan, and though he wasn't baptized until he was on his deathbed (a common practice at the time to keep one from having the chance to sin again before death), he was a patron of the Church and the institution thrived under his reign.

**A bust of Constantine**

Constantine made a second major change when he chose a small town called Byzantium as his new capital. Located at the juncture between Europe and Asia on a promontory on the Bosphorus, it was easily defended and well situated to rule over the Eastern half of the empire. In addition to controlling the trade route between the Black Sea and the Mediterranean, it was also the western outlet for the Silk Route. Constantine renamed his new capital Constantinople and stripped the wealth of a dozen cities to adorn its public spaces. Statues and bas-reliefs from across the Roman world adorned luxurious palaces and squares, and a giant Hippodrome hosted chariot races while being overlooked by a huge statue of Constantine atop a 100 foot column of porphyry. At the center of the city stood a four-sided arch topped by the True Cross, supposedly discovered by Constantine's mother Helena when she visited the Holy Land.

 The old capital at Rome was already in decline, and this shift of focus to the east had long-lasting consequences. By the end of the 4th century, Constantinople was already eclipsing Rome in wealth and influence, although the Eternal City still remained a potent symbol. Many fine churches had sprung up now that Christianity enjoyed the patronage of the nobility and a succession of emperors, but even so, the Western Roman emperors were now ruling from Milan, which was closer to the troubled provinces across the Alps such as Gaul. These emperors were increasingly weak, with the wealthy families and bishops expanding their power in local areas as the central government struggled to contain the troubled situation.

Even the rule of Constantine didn't stop the pressure at the empire's periphery, and more and more, the emperors in the West and East ruled their separate affairs with little or no consultation or assistance from the other half of the empire. It was becoming increasingly clear that the Roman Empire was splitting in two.

Theodosius, who ruled from 379-395 CE, was the last emperor to truly rule an undivided empire. At first, he became emperor only of the East after taking over from his predecessor, Valens, who was killed at the disastrous defeat at the hands of the Goths and their barbarian allies at the Battle of Adrianople in 378 CE. At that battle, an entire army was wiped out, but Theodosius continued the campaign until it ground to a standstill. Eventually, peace was established by settling the invaders in Illyricum south of the Danube, showing once again that turning enemies into allies was one of the Romans' most effective tactics.

**A depiction of Theodosius holding a laurel wreath in a relief on the Hippodrome in Constantinople**

In 392 CE, the Emperor of the West, Valentinian II, was found hanged in his palace, and though his generals claimed the emperor killed himself, Theodosius wasn't convinced. He became more suspicious when they proclaimed Eugenius, a pagan, as emperor. Fearing a pagan coup in the West, Theodosius named his eight-year-old son Honorius as emperor and marched with an army to secure the claim in 394 CE. He was successful and for a brief time ruled the entire empire, but upon his death in 395 CE, the empire was again divided into eastern and western halves. The more important eastern half went to his older son Arcadius, while the shambles in the West went to his younger son Honorius. The western half would continue to decay while the eastern half developed into what was later known as the Byzantine Empire.

Since most of the peoples and/or tribes that participated in the migrations and/or invasions of Europe during the early common era were Germanic in origin, the modern study of these peoples and period has taken on a decidedly German character, and terms, such as the *Völkerwanderung,* have gained widespread acceptance in the modern academic lexicon (Goffart 2006, 13). Unfortunately, since the various tribes were, for the most part, illiterate when they began their treks into and throughout Europe, the Latin and Greek primary sources that recorded their activities were quite negligible until about the fifth century CE (Goffart 2006, 19). Also, because these sources were written by chroniclers loyal to Rome and Byzantium, they were often biased and hostile towards the Vandals, who they rightfully saw as enemies of their own people. Because of the dearth of primary sources regarding the early details of the migrations, modern scholars are left to guess what, exactly, caused the mass movement of peoples that disrupted and ultimately played a major factor in the collapse of the Roman Empire. Although the precise reasons may never be known, many scholars believe that the appearance of the Asiatic Huns in Europe in the late fourth century CE precipitated the movements, proving to be the proverbial straw that broke the camel's back (Goffart 2006, 21). After the Huns arrived in Europe, they set into motion a domino effect of more migrations creating hostility and warfare among the Germanic tribes and pushing them further into the confines of Roman territory. At first glance, the mass migrations into and throughout Europe in the early common era may seem chaotic and confusing, but a closer look reveals that the movements were actually quite organized.

Although there were scores of different tribes that participated in the migrations, modern scholars have divided the Germanic peoples into two categories–West and East Germans. The West Germans originated somewhere in Eastern Europe and pressed westward from between the Oder and Elbe rivers until they displaced the more culturally sophisticated, but less warlike Celts, east of the Rhine, and north of the Main rivers, around 200 BC (Bury 1967, 5). The West Germans, perhaps influenced by the Celts who they replaced, adopted a more sedentary lifestyle and culture, and farming and cooperation with the Romans became common. It was to these Germans that Julius Caesar and the Roman historian, Tacitus, would dedicate much of their writings (Bury 1967, 7). The amount of pressure the West Germans placed on the Roman Empire was negligible, but their cousins, the East Germans, entered the scene later with much more bluster and violence.

The East Germans migrated into continental Europe from Scandinavia sometime between 600 and 300 BC (Bury 1967, 5), and almost immediately proved to be much more of a problem for the Romans than their West German cousins. The Vandals, along with the Goths and Gepids, were the most notable of the East German tribes, who early in their migrations followed a southerly track that took them to the shores of the Black Sea and the banks of the Danube River by the third and fourth centuries CE (Bury 1967, 15). The migrations appear to have followed an organized pattern, at least from the perspective of the Germanic tribes, which is further confirmed by the sophisticated styles of government they followed during the period.

As people in both Rome and Constantinople jockeyed for position, trouble was brewing among the Visigoths. As the Romans were sorting out there problems, the Visigoths had settled in Thrace and the Ostrogoths in Gratian's part of Illyricum, but this did not denote the end of the Goths' raiding activity. Theodosius defeated the Ostrogoth marauders in 388, but the Visigoths continued to raid Illyricum for several years after his death in 395. By 400, the Visigoths had pushed into Spain, so the Balkans was left to the Ostrogoths.

The most prominent of the many Germanic leaders of this time was Alaric, king of the Visigoths. While he had served Theodosius loyally and led the Visigothic part of the Roman army to victory against the Western Roman Emperor Eugenius at the Battle of the River Frigidus in 394 CE, he was not rewarded for this service with any sort of high office or a generalship, and this undoubtedly rankled him. In effect, Theodosius had won the entire Roman Empire and Alaric essentially got nothing.

Alaric's own people, however, adored him and raised him up as their king in 395. The historian Jordanes noted, "When Alaric was proclaimed king, he held an assembly of the people and persuaded them to seek a kingdom through their own endeavors instead of passively serving others." At the time, the Visigoths were not one united people but an ethnic group with many different divisions that are still poorly understood by modern historians. Thus, while his contemporaries referred to Alaric as a "king," this title may exaggerate his actual power. Indeed, Alaric faced many challenges to his rule from other Visigoth leaders over the course of his life.

Zosimus wrote that Rufinus heard of Alaric's plans for finding a homeland and encouraged him to head west, promising easier pickings and that the Eastern Roman army would help: "Rufinus, therefore, privately communicated with him, prompting him to lead forth his barbarians, and auxiliaries of any other nation, as he might with ease render himself master of the whole country. Alaric on this marched out of Thrace into

Macedon and Thessaly, committing the greatest devastations on his way. Upon approaching Thermopylae, he privately sent messengers to Antiochus the proconsul, and to Gerontius the governor of the garrison at Thermopylae, to inform them of his approach. This news was no sooner communicated to Gerontius than he and the garrison retired and left the barbarians a free passage into Greece. Upon arriving there, they immediately began to pillage the country and to sack all the towns, killing all the men, both young and old, and carrying off the women and children, together with the money. In this incursion, all Boeotia, and whatever countries of Greece the barbarians passed through after their entrance at Thermopylae, were so ravaged, that the traces are visible to the present day."

Greece was part of the Eastern Roman Empire, so it seems Rufinus' plan backfired. Nonetheless, Stilicho decided to head off Alaric before he made it to the West by sailing with an army to Greece. At first he was successful, but it appears he was ordered out of Eastern Roman territory before he could finish off the Visigoths.

Frustrated, Stilicho had Rufinus assassinated, but unfortunately for the Western half's regent, Rufinus was soon replaced by the eunuch Eutropius, and Stilicho was faced with an even craftier enemy. Zosimus wrote, "Eutropius, being intoxicated with wealth, and elevated in his own imagination above the clouds, planted his emissaries in almost every country, to pry into the conduct of affairs, and the circumstances of every individual; nor was there any thing from which he did not derive some profit."

Eutropius settled Alaric and his people in Dacia and raised the leader to the status of general. It was then that he got Gildo to rebel in North Africa, but Rome's Senate still outranked the one in Constantinople. Furthermore, it was the Roman senators who would be hurt by social instability if the grain shipments to Rome were stopped. For centuries, these shipments had been crucial to keep the urban rabble in line, and whenever these shipments had been disrupted, rioting was not far behind. Thus, the Senate declared war on Gildo and branded Eutropius an outlaw.

When Gildo was defeated, Eutropius' star began to wane. He was blamed for a disastrous campaign against the Ostrogoths in Asia Minor and for his political machinations, so when the people's hate overcame their fears, Eutropius was killed in 400. That same year, Stilicho was raised to consul.

It seems remarkable that the emperors and their courts would spend so much time, money, men, and energy fighting each other when the borders were hemorrhaging and barbarian tribes were migrating through Roman provinces, but one of the fatal flaws of the Roman mentality was an overweening pride. Romans simply could not accept the possibility that barbarians could outfight or outthink them. If a Roman army was defeated, it must have been by treachery, and if a barbarian tribe asked to negotiate terms of a treaty, those terms could be casually ignored. Time and again, the Visigoths offered peace, providing a chance for the Romans to strengthen their empire with vital new blood, but time and again Roman pride and conniving kept them from saving themselves.

Alaric soon decided to restart his migration to the West. He may have been encouraged by plotters in Constantinople, or he may simply have realized he could have more land in the more unstable Western

Roman Empire, but either way, he and his people set out in 401. By that winter, he was camped in the region of Venetia, modern Venice, and this caused a panic in Italy. Stilicho was along the Danube fighting an invasion by the Ostrogoths, Honorius appeared mentally paralyzed, and little seems to have been done to stop the Visigoths either by force or diplomacy.

When Alaric moved towards Honorius' capital at Milan the following spring, the young emperor moved his capital to Ravenna in northern Italy. This heavily fortified city had the additional protection of a ring of marshes that hampered any approach of siege engines, and only a narrow road led to the city. It was also an important naval base, so if the walls were breached, Honorius could sail to safety. That said, while it provided a secure refuge for much of the emperor's reign, its marginal location meant that Honorius was often out of touch with events elsewhere on the peninsula.

As it turned out, the defenses of Ravenna would not need to be tested after Stilicho defeated the Ostrogoths and hurried back to Italy, where he called for legions from Britain to join him. The Visigoths retreated west to the Alps, and Stilicho was able to run them down on April 6, 402 at Pollentia and hand them a serious defeat. Alaric's own family was captured in the battle.

Despite this setback, Alaric continued his campaign. The following year, Stilicho defeated him again outside Verona, but both armies were seriously depleted from the hard campaign and Alaric and Stilicho came to an understanding: Alaric would leave Italy and settle in Illyricum on the eastern fringes of the Western Roman Empire. It is widely believed by historians that Stilicho tempted Alaric not only with lands but the chance to fight the Eastern Emperor for more loot, which indicates Stilicho hadn't given up his plotting against the East.

Back in Rome, the deal was spun as a major victory, and the masses believed Stilicho had saved Italy. Honorius, of course, took credit too, and the emperor celebrated "his" victory by staging a triumphal entry into Rome in 404. The court poet Claudian wrote that the women of Rome swooned at the appearance of the emperor, now a handsome young man of 19 wearing his bejeweled regalia: "The roar of the adoring multitude. . .rises up like thunder from the hollow bowl of the arena, reverberating round the seven hills to echo back as one the name 'Honorius'. Here in the circus military displays, too, are staged. Here we can often see armed squadrons fan out and advance, wheel round and fall back again in perfect order and tight discipline; a fine display. A thrilling artifice of war. The master sounds the order with his whip. In perfect unison, the massed ranks perform their new maneuvers, clashing their shields against their sides or shaking them above their heads; the round shields resonate low, the swords ring sharp and clear, creating a symphony, a rhythmic beating, with swords and shields in harmony. As one, the phalanx kneels. A sea of helmets bows in salute before you, our leader. Then the troops split and spiral, running out in well-rehearsed formation. . .they wheel apart again and coil back in tight formation."

While Claudian was undoubtedly exaggerating Honorius' popularity, the crowd certainly did have reason to celebrate. There had been too few victories of late, and this severe defeat of Rome's enemy was a boost to public morale. Living as they were in the Eternal City, it was easy for them to feel that things may have been turning around; Rome was still the largest city in the world with an estimated population of about 800,000 and while the hinterland saw bad times, there was a flurry of building in Rome itself. Public and much private money was no longer going to pagan temples. They remained open and many remained impressive, but others were falling in to disrepair. Instead, large amounts of money went to church building.

The standard building type for churches was the basilica, colonnaded buildings with an apse that were used for many years in the empire as meeting halls that the clergy saw as tailor-made for a religious community. Existing basilicas were turned into houses of worship, while others were specially built as churches. Santa Maria Maggiore is one of these specially built basilicas, commissioned by Pope Sixtus III (ruled 432-440 CE). The interior of Santa Maria Maggiore is well preserved and gives a good idea of a wealthy church of its day. It is Classical in style, with golden mosaics on the walls. Notably, the Virgin Mary is dressed like a Roman empress.

Paganism was still alive, however, and even Honorius, a patron of the church and in close contact with the Pope, felt the need to pour a libation to the river god of the Tiber when he made his triumphal entry into Rome. Furthermore, many Romans gave lip service to the new Christian faith while still privately worshipping the old gods. In the Roman mind this wasn't hypocrisy but merely the syncretism of a polytheistic faith. Over time, however, stricter rules against pagan practice came into place, and the fact that rulers as late as the end of the 6th century were still trying to stamp out paganism shows how much it endured in Roman and early medieval minds.

Of course, the victory celebration was short lived, because soon after, the Ostrogoths once again crossed the Danube, marched all the way to Italy, and besieged Florence. By this time, the Roman army was sapped of its strength after so many years of fighting, so the Romans resorted to desperate measures. Soldiers' pay was increased to encourage enlistment, slaves were offered their freedom if they would fight for Rome, and Stilicho even recruited Huns (some of whom became his personal bodyguard). The desperate measures paid off in August 406, when Stilicho decisively defeated the Ostrogoths. The Ostrogothic king died in battle, and 12,000 of his warriors were taken prisoner. Stilicho, still desperate for troops, offered them a place in the

Roman army, which they gladly accepted. As such, fewer and fewer of the fighting men in the Roman Empire were actually Roman.

However, things were going badly elsewhere in the Western Roman Empire. That winter was terribly fierce, with temperatures so low that the Rhine froze over. The Vandals, Alans, Suevi, and Burgundians clustered on the east bank, and seeing their chance to flee the Huns, swarmed over the ice and spread through Germania and Gaul, leaving a vast swath of destruction in their wake. The bishop Orientius of Auch, who was living in Gaul at the time, wrote that "the skies were thick with smoke as all of Gaul burned on one pyre."

On the furthest fringes of the empire, there was even more trouble. Britannia had been stripped of most of its troops to fight Alaric, and now it was facing increased attacks from Saxon pirates raiding from northern Germany. It was also fighting off incursions from the Picts and Scots. The remaining soldiers, frustrated at lack of support from Rome, raised three different men to lead, but only the third, Constantine III, was able to assert any authority. While the usurper Constantine III had been declared emperor to protect Britannia in 407, he actually did the opposite. He felt that the island was lost, and that it was better to protect the richer lands of Gaul, so he stripped the last of the troops from Britannia and sailed for the mainland. An army sent by Stilicho wasn't able to stop him, and soon he had established himself in Gaul, securing the Rhine and being recognized by the local people. Just how low the empire had sunk can be seen in the fact that Stilicho's general, retreating back to Italy, had to bribe the bandits who controlled the Alpine passes to let him cross.

**An ancient coin depicting Constantine III**

Instead of clearing out the barbarians ravaging the countryside, Constantine III invaded Hispania in order to defeat Honorius' cousins based there, and he further secured his position after capturing two of them. However, Constantine's position was merely set on sand; although no more barbarians were crossing the Rhine at the moment, those who already had made it across during the harsh winter ran loose in the countryside and would soon march into Hispania looking for fresh lands to plunder.

All the while, these events severely undercut Stilicho's reputation as a protector of the empire. His daughter Maria, Honorius' wife, died, and Stilicho hurriedly got the emperor to marry another of his daughters, Thermantia. While he was once again the emperor's father-in-law, he still couldn't control the rapidly decaying situation. Alaric, left alone in Illyricum and now seeing that the anticipated invasion of the Eastern Roman Empire wasn't going to take place, marched again on Italy in 408. Alaric demanded compensation for dragging his people back and forth across the empire, and he was able to get a promise of 4,000 pounds of gold. With the Senate and the people loudly complaining, Stilicho tried to shift the blame for this by saying the invasion of the East was Honorius' idea. The emperor was insulted; no longer a child, Honorius began to assert his will and was increasingly mistrustful of his father-in-law.

Events accelerated later that year. Some of the troops in Italy mutinied, but when Stilicho quashed the rebellion and ordered the leaders executed, Honorius countermanded that order. The emperor was obviously trying to win over troops that he would need in a showdown with Stilicho. He had heard that Arcadius, the Emperor of the East, had died, and the 7 year old Theodosius II had been proclaimed emperor. Of course the boy was a puppet of the eastern court, and both Honorius and Stilicho wanted to gain control over him. Honorius wanted to sail to Constantinople, but Stilicho said he should be the one who should go, claiming it would be too dangerous and expensive for the emperor to go himself. Honorius tried to dissuade Stilicho and in the end neither went.

By this time, they had too much to take care of at home. One of Stilicho's rivals at the western court, the eunuch Olympius, saw his chance. Emboldened by the general's weakened position, he began to spread rumors that Stilicho was planning to go east, overthrow Theodosius II, and put his son Eucherius in his place. Olympius also outmaneuvered Stilicho among Honorius' men. Honorius was giving a speech to his army near Milan just before it was setting out to fight

Constantine III, but Olympius had the troops kill their leaders and seemingly begin to riot. Honorius, surprisingly enough, rose to the task and went among the rampaging soldiers, managing to pacify them, and when Stilicho heard of this from his camp in Bologna, he marched with his troops to Ravenna, purportedly to help Honorius crush the revolt and punish its leaders. While on the march, a team of Goths led by the general Sarus slipped into the camp at night, killed Stilicho's Hunnish bodyguards, and almost captured the general himself. Stilicho managed to get away, but he was caught in Ravenna by Olympius' soldiers and put to the sword. One of the last powerful leaders of the Western Roman Empire was dead.

**A medieval illustration depicting the Visigoths and Rome**

After Stilicho's death, Olympius ordered a purge of everyone who had been associated with Stilicho. Many leading officials were tortured and killed, and their property was confiscated by the state. Honorius also wanted to distance himself from the dead general, so he divorced Thermantia. Thermantia was his second and last wife, so he never had any children. In the meantime, the Imperial troops used this toxic atmosphere as an opportunity to get revenge on the *foederati*, the barbarian troops loyal to Stilicho. Unable or unwilling to attack their camp, they instead attacked their homes, slaughtering, burning, and looting. This compelled some 30,000 *foederati* to immediately switch allegiance to Alaric, who was again approaching Italy. He had never received the 4,000 pounds of gold he had been promised and knew that promise had died with Stilicho. Now Alaric was after a greater prize: the city of Rome.

Alaric marched through Italy all but unopposed, and after the defection of the *foederati*, there was no significant force to stop him. Honorius and his court stayed in Ravenna, fearing a siege, but Alaric marched by and continued south, and with that, his goal soon became apparent. By October 408, the Visigoths had surrounded the ancient Roman capital, and they quickly seized Portus, Rome's port at the mouth of the Tiber River. The city had always relied on regular grain shipments to feed its massive population, and without them, starvation wasn't far away. As a result, the city authorities cut the grain handouts in half in order to buy time.

The citizens of Rome waited to be saved by their emperor, but Honorius and his court in Ravenna did nothing. Soon the grain issue was cut to a third, and even when leading citizens doled out their personal stocks, but it wasn't nearly enough. Soon the people began to starve, and rumors of cannibalism spread through the frightened streets. Zosimus wrote, "the famine, as might be expected, was succeeded by a pestilence, and all places were filled with dead bodies. As the dead could not be interred outside the city, for the enemy was in possession of all the avenues, the city was made their sepulcher. Thus it was in danger of being depopulated by an additional cause, and though no want of provisions had subsisted, yet the stench arising from the putrid corpses was sufficient to infect them with disease."

The Senate became desperate, and after hearing no word from Honorius, it decided to take matters into its own hands by sending envoys to Alaric. Zosimus explained:

"They then resolved on sending an embassy to the enemy, to inform him that they were willing to accept any reasonable conditions of peace, and at the same time were ready for war, since the people of Rome had taken up arms, and by means of continual military exercise were become well disposed for action.

"Basilius was appointed their ambassador, who was a Spaniard, and governor of a province. Johannes, the chief of the imperial notaries, went with him, because he was acquainted with Alaric, and might be the cause of a reconciliation. The Romans did not certainly know whether Alaric himself was present or not, or whether it was he who besieged the city. For they were deluded by a report that it was another person, who had been a friend of Stilico, which had occasioned him to come against their city.

"When the ambassadors came to him, they were ashamed of the ignorance in which the Romans had so long remained, but delivered the message of the Senate. When Alaric heard it, and that the people having been exercised to arms were ready for war, he remarked, 'The thickest grass is easier to cut than the thinnest.'

"Having said this, he laughed immoderately at the ambassadors. But when they spoke of peace, he used such expressions as were in the extreme of arrogance and presumption. He declared, that he would not relinquish the siege on any condition but that of receiving all the gold and silver in the city, all the household goods, and the barbarian slaves. One of the ambassadors observing, 'If you take all these, what will you leave for the citizens?' He replied, 'Their Souls.'

". . .After long discussions on both sides, it was at length agreed, that the city should give five thousand pounds of gold, and thirty thousand of silver, four thousand silk robes, three thousand scarlet fleeces, and three thousand pounds of pepper."

The demand of pepper may seem unusual compared to the others, but pepper came from India and was thus a highly prized and expensive, condiment. It was probably worth more than its weight in silver.

Since the Imperial treasury was in Ravenna with Honorius, the senators had to raise the money themselves, yet even in this extreme situation, many thought more of themselves than their city and tried to hide their wealth. When the amount gathered proved woefully short, the senators turned on the ancient pagan temples, stripping the statues of their precious metals and melting down many solid gold and silver figurines.

Meanwhile, at Ravenna in December 408, a party from Constantine III appeared in order to confer with Honorius. The usurper asked for the emperor's official pardon for claiming to be emperor, but since he had no major force to protect him at this time, Honorius went one further by recognizing Constantine III as co-emperor. It's unclear why he did this, but historians figure he either wanted a loyal ally in a world where he had none or perhaps wanted someone else to share his unbearable burden.

While that was happening, the Senate in Rome sent envoys to Ravenna to inform the emperor of the deal they had made and asked for his formal ratification.

Alaric also sent offers of a peace treaty that included an exchange of child hostages for each side to hold (a common form of insurance at the time), which would in turn bring Alaric and his army onto the side of Rome to fight the other barbarian incursions. When Honorius agreed, Alaric then lifted the siege for three days, allowing ships moored at Pontus to release their cargos. The people of Rome gratefully sat down to eat. At the same time, many slaves used the opportunity to flee the city and join Alaric's army.

  Once those three days were up, the siege resumed, with the agreement that it would be lifted permanently once the hostages from Honorius arrived, but they never did. As the Visigoths waited with increasing impatience, food supplies within the city once again became critically low. Again, the Senate sent envoys to Ravenna begging Honorius to fulfill his side of the bargain, but the emperor was cowed by the eunuch Olympius, who for unknown reasons disapproved of the agreement. Thus, instead of sending the hostages and securing peace and perhaps a powerful ally, Honorius sent five legions from Dalmatia instead, only for Alaric's forces to ambush them in a mountain pass and wipe them out. About 100 soldiers made it to Rome.

Yet another group of envoys was sent to Ravenna, this time including Pope Innocent I (ruled 402-417), and the situation was becoming critical. Alaric's brother-in-law Athavulf (meaning "noble wolf" in Gothic) had appeared in northern Italy with a second Visigothic army, but instead of making peace, Honorius sent Olympius with 300 Huns in the service of the Imperial court to fight them. They made a successful nighttime raid against Athavulf's camp, but the army was too large to defeat and Olympius was forced to retreat. He returned to Ravenna only to be removed from office, a victim of the court intrigue that he had so avidly participated in. He fled to Dalmatia, leaving the sinking ship.

More chaos ensued when the garrison at the port of Ravenna mutinied, cutting off food supplies in the current capital. While Honorius hid, the praetorian prefect Jovius calmed the mutineers, which has led some historians to believe the mutiny was stage-managed by Jovius himself, taking a cue from the military riot staged by Olympius.

Either way, a grateful Honorius was once again under the sway of a court schemer, and Jovius invited Alaric and Athavulf to Ravenna for peace talks, but the Visigoths refused to come. Instead, they suggested meeting at Rimini, away from the Imperial court, its intrigue, and its weak-willed emperor. Alaric reiterated his demands for a homeland and money, and Jovius sent a letter back to the emperor with these terms, and also included a letter suggesting Honorius raise Alaric to the rank of *Magister Utriusque Militiae* ("Master of Both Forces", i.e. both the infantry and cavalry), the same prominent military office once held by Stilicho. This would establish Alaric high in the Imperial hierarchy and hopefully ensure his loyalty.

   When the response came, Jovius made one of the great missteps of history. Confident that Honorius would do the right thing, he had the letters read aloud in Alaric's presence without vetting them first. Honorius' reply stated that while he agreed to the money and land, he said in lofty tones that he would never give Alaric any sort of official position. Alaric immediately marched back to Rome. Jovius, in a bid to save face, went to Ravenna with a bellicose air and swore by placing his hand on Honorius' head that he would never make peace with the Visigoths.

Zosimus wrote of this lost opportunity:

"Affairs having thus been concerted, the emperor called ten thousand Huns to his assistance in the war against Alaric. In order that he might have provisions ready for them on their arrival, he ordered the Dalmatians to bring corn, sheep, and oxen. He sent out scouts to gain information of the way by which Alaric intended to march to Rome.

"But Alaric, in the meantime, repented of his intention of proceeding against Rome, and sent the bishops of each city, not only as ambassadors, but also to advise the emperor not to suffer so noble a city, which for more than a thousand years had ruled over a great part of the world, to be seized and destroyed by the barbarians, nor such magnificent edifices to be demolished by hostile flames, but to prefer entering into a peace on some reasonable conditions.

"He instructed them to state to the emperor, that the barbarians wanted no preferments, nor did he now desire the provinces which he had previously chosen as his residence, but only the two Norica, which are situated on the extremity of the river Danube, are harassed by continual incursions, and yield to the treasury a very small revenue. Besides this be only demanded annually as much corn as the emperor should think proper to grant, and would remit the gold. And that a friendship and alliance should subsist between himself and the Romans, against every one that should rise to oppose the empire.

"When Alaric had made these extremely temperate propositions, his moderation being universally admired, Jovius, and the other ministers of the emperor, declared that his demands could not possibly be acceded to, since all persons, who held any commission, had sworn not to make peace with Alaric. For if their oath had been made to the deity, they might indeed probably have dispensed with it, and have relied on the divine goodness for pardon; but since they had sworn by the head of the emperor, it was by no means lawful for them to infringe so great a vow. So cautious were they who then held the chief management of affairs, as they were destitute of the care and protection of heaven."

Alaric had one final card to play by appealing to the Roman Senate to overrule Honorius and act on its own to save the city. To tighten the screws, Alaric reoccupied Portus and also the older port of Ostia and took all the grain in the warehouses for himself. The senators invited Alaric to come to the Senate itself to discuss matters, and Alaric must have been confident he would be safe, presumably because if he had been harmed, his people would let the city starve. He appeared before the Senate on November 3, 409 in a Roman toga trimmed with imperial purple, and he now had a new demand: the Senate had do depose Honorius and put the prefect of the city of Rome, Priscus Attalus, in his place. The prefect had intervened several times in the past two years in an effort to get Honorius to accede to Alaric's demands, and the Visigothic leader obviously saw the prefect as, if not a friend, at least one of those rare Romans who would listen to reason.

The Senate immediately obliged. They had had enough of their ineffective emperor, and Priscus Attalus was a senator who respected the traditions of the Senate and, having been raised to the purple by it, would be sure to guard its interests. Priscus Attalus was a pagan, so the first thing that needed to be done was to get him baptized by an Arian bishop to match his faith with that of Alaric's. The following day, he spoke to the Senate as the new emperor, and as expected, he promised to respect the traditions and office of the Senate and boasted that soon it would control both halves of the Roman Empire.

**A coin depicting Priscus Attalus**

Despite this seemingly momentous chain of events, Priscus Attalus was not truly the emperor of the Roman Empire, nor even the Western Roman Empire. If anything, Priscus Attalus was merely the emperor of the city of Rome and whatever land Alaric then controlled; anything else would have to be fought over. Nevertheless, he was acclaimed in the streets by a populace once again allowed to eat, and he named Alaric as *Magister Utriusque Militium*, or commander-in-chief, while Athavulf became commander of the household cavalry.

The main problem facing the new power in Rome was that the city's vital grain supply came from Africa, and Africa was controlled by Heraclian, a man Honorius had appointed. Alaric wanted to send his Visigoths to invade, but Priscus Attalus decided on diplomacy and sent a delegation to Carthage.

In the meantime, the Visigoths marched north and met a delegation from Honorius at Rimini. The emperor at Ravenna was willing to recognize Priscus Attalus in exchange for peace, but the usurper at Rome felt that having three emperors in the West meant that no one would wield true power and the infighting would inevitably continue. Instead, Priscus Attalus sent a message to Honorius offering to spare his life if he went into exile, and Honorius might have accepted if not for the envoy adding the stipulation that he be mutilated in the right hand. The right hand was the one the emperor raised in order to make his proclamations official, so mutilation would mean he could never rule again. Honorius refused.

Adding to the drama, Honorius subsequently got some unexpected help from Constantinople in the form of 4,000 elite Eastern troops. The court of his nephew, Theodosius II, had finally decided to answer his repeated calls for aid, and Honorius also got news from North Africa that Heraclian remained loyal. He had killed the ambassador Priscus Attalus had sent and put an embargo on all ships headed to Rome. In response, Priscus Attalus sent a Roman army to fight Heraclian, and though he could have sent a much larger Visigothic force, he wanted to be his own man and not a puppet of the barbarians. However, when his army was defeated, a frustrated Alaric marched his men around Italy, bringing cities and towns into the fold and taking their excess food to feed Rome's discontent mob.

Despite Alaric's efforts, it was not nearly enough. People were dying in the streets and a rumor went around that a crowd had gathered in the Circus

Maximus chanting, "Put a price on human flesh!" Desperate, Alaric once again marched along the well-worn road to Ravenna, bringing Priscus Attalus with him. The usurper was stripped of his imperial regalia, which was sent to Honorius as a gift, and Honorius looked eager to sign a peace treaty, but this last hope for an agreement was foiled when Sarus, Alaric's Visigothic rival and now a hanger-on at the court in Ravenna, snuck out with 300 men and attacked Alaric's camp. It was just a raid, but it destroyed any chance for peace. Alaric assumed Honorius had sent the raiders. Enraged, he turned back towards Rome, ready to truly teach the Romans a lesson.

On August 24, 410, the unthinkable happened. For 800 years, the Eternal City had stood untouched as the shining and invincible symbol of Roman greatness. That day, Alaric and his men were camped outside of the Salarian Gate, one of the many gates among the formidable walls of the city that Honorius had strengthened just a few years before. The gate, like all the others, was shut tight, and the municipal garrison manned the walls.

Then, inexplicably, the gate opened, and no one knows

for sure who opened the gate or why. Ancient chroniclers tell different stories, and none of the surviving accounts from that day were written by eyewitnesses. Some say it was a Roman traitor hoping for clemency from the barbarians, while others claim that Alaric sent soldiers in under the guise of being slaves, and that they subsequently overcame the guards at the Salarian Gate and opened it.

Whoever did it, the Visigoths were ready for the moment, and when it opened, they charged through the gate and headed for various points in the city. Each group had their own objective; all were under strict orders not to engage in wholesale pillage or slaughter, and all church property was off-limits.

Their first target was the Gardens of Sallust, close to the Salarian Gate. This was a large complex of sumptuous palaces and pleasure gardens, some of them dating as far back as the 1st century B.C. The palaces were richly decorated with precious metals and jewels, and the gardens adorned with Classical statues, all of which were taken or destroyed and the palaces burned.

While the Christian Visigoths protected the churches, not all the Christians were safe. St. Augustine, who wrote about the sack in his famous book *City of God*, wrote that "many Christians were slaughtered, and were put to death in a hideous variety of cruel ways." This may be attributed to warriors being overcome by rage during the looting - soldiers of all faiths and eras have done terrible things to helpless populations throughout history - and also the sizeable number of pagans in the ranks who had no sympathies for the new religion.

St. Jerome (c. 347-420), in a letter to the devout young Christian woman Principia, tells of how the Visigoths came to the monastic community of Marcella, a leading noblewoman who had devoted her life and wealth to her faith after the death of her husband. It was housed in Marcella's old palace, which had been stripped of its valuables when she had donated them all to the Church. Jerome wrote:

> "One of the bloodstained victors found his way into Marcella's house. Now be it mine to say what I have heard, to relate what holy men have seen; for there were some such present and they say that you too were with her in the hour of danger. When the soldiers entered she is said to have received them without any look of

alarm; and when they asked her for gold she pointed to her coarse dress to show them that she had no buried treasure.

"However they would not believe in her self-chosen poverty, but scourged her and beat her with cudgels. She is said to have felt no pain but to have thrown herself at their feet and to have pleaded with tears for you, that you might not be taken from her, or owing to your youth have to endure what she as an old woman had no occasion to fear.

"Christ softened their hard hearts and even among bloodstained swords natural affection asserted its rights. The barbarians conveyed both you and her to the basilica of the apostle Paul, that you might find there either a place of safety or, if not that, at least a tomb. Hereupon Marcella is said to have burst into great joy and to have thanked God for having kept you unharmed in answer to her prayer. She said she was thankful too that the taking of the city had found her poor, not made her so, that she was now in want of daily bread, that Christ satisfied her needs so that she no longer felt hunger, that she was able to say in word and in deed: 'naked came I out of my mother's womb, and naked shall I return thither: the Lord gave and the Lord hath taken away; blessed be the name of the Lord.'"

Marcella died from her beating a few days later.

Groups of marauders targeted several other major palaces and public buildings, and high on the Visigoths' list were landmarks that had symbolic importance to the Romans, such as the Mausoleums of Augustus and Hadrian, which housed the cremated remains of several emperors and their noble families. The ashes were tossed out into the street, but the buildings left relatively untouched; what was important was the disrespect shown to the greatest figures of Roman history.

Of course, chaos reigned throughout the city, and while those who crowded into churches appear to have been left unharmed, many who for whatever reasons did not or could not get to a church were often attacked. There were tales of slaves getting revenge on their masters and joining in the looting, and of women hauled away to the slave markets. Some citizens were able to slip through the Visigothic blockade and sail away to refuges such as the nearby island of Igilium, but they were few and far between.

Later writers mentioned many tales of clemency, stories of brave nuns who shamed Visigothic looters into sparing church artifacts, or chaste Roman matrons who fought so hard against their assailants that the men left them unharmed. In hindsight, it's likely that these Christian chroniclers felt the need to downplay the cruelty of the sack in order to explain how a pagan city that stood untouched for centuries could be looted by a Christian army so soon after embracing the new faith. St. Augustine wrote his *City of God* to solve this tricky theological problem and put forth that any city built by man was by its very nature flawed, and therefore nothing compared to the ideal city in heaven.

**An illustration depicting Alaric entering Rome**

After three days, the Visigoths were done, and it was understandably why they left since there was no food and the bodies littering the streets filled the city with an unbearable stench. With winter coming, the Visigoths also had to find a place to settle with enough food to feed their vast numbers, so they headed south, hoping to take ships to North Africa, the breadbasket of the empire. As they went, they ransacked more cities and country estates, taking any valuables and food they could find. They reached Rhegium, at the tip of Italy's "toe", and assembled a large fleet to take them across the Mediterranean.

However, the sea gets increasingly rough in the region as summer turns to autumn, and in ancient times it was dangerous to sail in winter. Alaric launched a first group of ships to test the rough waters and they all sank, so the Visigoths were trapped in Italy for the winter. It was also around this time that Alaric himself fell ill. Jordanes noted: "Alaric was cast down by his reverse and, while deliberating what he should do, was suddenly overtaken by an untimely death and departed from human cares. His people mourned for him with the utmost affection. Then turning from its course the river Busentus near the city of Consentia--for this stream flows with its wholesome waters from the foot of a mountain near that city--they led a band of captives into the midst of its bed to dig out a place for his grave. In the depths of this pit they buried Alaric, together with many treasures, and then turned the waters back into their channel. And that none might ever know the place, they put to death all the diggers. They bestowed the kingdom of the Visigoths on Athavulf his kinsman, a man of imposing beauty and great spirit; for though not tall of stature, he was distinguished for beauty of face and form."

## The Fall of the Western Roman Empire

The sack of Rome in 410, although fairly mild by ancient standards, was a major blow to Roman morale, and Honorius has gone down in history as one of the worst Roman emperors, blamed by his contemporaries and later historians alike for not providing strong leadership during the crisis. The 6th century Byzantine historian Procopius, in his *Vandalic War*, gives this anecdote: "At that time they say that the Emperor Honorius in Ravenna received the message from one of the eunuchs, evidently a keeper of the poultry, that Rome had perished. And he cried out and said, 'And yet it has just eaten from my hands!' For he had a very large cock, Rome by name; and the eunuch comprehending his words said that it was the city of Rome which had perished at the hands of Alaric, and the emperor with a sigh of relief answered quickly: 'But

I thought that my fowl Rome had perished.' So great, they say, was the folly with which this emperor was possessed." While the veracity of this story is obviously questionable, it speaks volumes about Honorius' legacy.

After burying his brother-in-law, Athavulf, now king of the Goths, led his people back up the Italian peninsula, sacking the countryside once again in order to feed his warriors and their families. They then passed over the Alps and into Gaul, which was no longer under Constantine III's control. Being named co-emperor in 408 had done little to stabilize his position; what should have been Constantine III's crowning glory was marred early the following year when he faced a usurper of his own in the form of his general Gerontius, along with increasing chaos thanks to the barbarians still at large in Gaul and now breaking into Hispania. Britannia also rebelled against him because its people had been left defenseless against their enemies.

Gerontius besieged Constantine III in Arles in 411, and Honorius sent an army to defeat them both. Honorius' troops defeated Gerontius' army and forced it to retreat, but they then continued the siege of Arles the usurper had started. Eventually, Constantine III surrendered on the agreement that his life would be spared, but he was betrayed and beheaded as he was being taken back to Ravenna.

In the wake of those events, it was now the Visigoths who swept through the war-torn province and took whatever they desired, but even at this late date, the Visigoths showed they were open to negotiation with Honorius. In 413, they defeated another usurper, Jovinus, in return for a promise of more food from Africa, but the food never came because Heraclian had rebelled. In 414, Athavulf raised Priscus Attalus to emperor like his predecessor Alaric had done, but this time a Roman force entered Gaul and captured the two-time usurper, hauling Priscus Attalus back to Rome. Honorius had Priscus Attalus' fingers of his right hand cut off, the same punishment that had once been suggested for Honorius himself.

Athavulf, disgusted at Roman duplicity, led his people south into Hispania, where he was assassinated by a rival in 415. The Visigoths, however, lived on, creating a kingdom that would endure until the Muslim invasion of the early 8th century.

Ironically, Honorius lasted longer than any of his rivals until dying of natural causes in 423, a rare privilege for a Rome emperor in that era, but later Roman emperors in the West found their waning power unequal to the task of holding the empire together. After the death of Honorius, a senior civil servant names Joannes became emperor, but the eastern emperor, Theodosius II, didn't approve and named his own man, Valentinian III, to the post. Valentinian III invaded the West and killed Joannes in 425, meaning Joannes had ruled less than two years. Valentinian III lasted until 455, seeing his power slowly wane and the Huns lay waste to much of the provinces. Large portions of North Africa, the Iberian peninsula, and Gaul were also lost to Germanic tribes.

Valentinian III was assassinated by a plot of senators, and he was succeeded by Petronius Maximus, who lasted less than three months before being stoned to death by an angry mob while fleeing Rome in the face of Geiseric the Vandal's approach to the city. The Vandals took Rome in 455 and sacked it for 14 days, looting it far more thoroughly than the Visigoths had a generation before.

The Western Roman Empire was now in its death throes. Nothing changed during the reign of the Emperor Avitus (ruled July 9, 455 – October 17, 456), who was quickly deposed. The next emperor, Majorian, was made of sterner stuff; although he lasted only until 461, he campaigned hard against the Visigoths and Vandals to retake some of the old empire. At this point, all that was left to him was Italy, Dalmatia, and part of Gaul. He managed to reconquer much of Gaul and Hispania, but he wasn't able to control his own *magister militum,* the Romanized German Ricimer, who was half Suevi and half Visigoth. Ricimer raised an army and defeated him. He then had the emperor tortured and beheaded, after which he installed the senator Libius Severus onto the throne.

The Western Empire now had only a few years to live. Libius Severus ruled until 465 but achieved little except the notable achievement of dying of natural causes. Anthemius came next, and he was backed by the Eastern emperor Leo I and thus less Ricimer's puppet. He launched vigorous campaigns against the Visigoths and Vandals and did much to improve relations with the East, but he was unequal to the task of dominating the intrigue in Ravenna. He was deposed and killed by

Ricimer in 472, who subsequently installed his own puppet, a man named Olybrius who died of dropsy after only seven months in office. By this time, Ricimer had also died, and his position had been taken over by his nephew Gundobad.

Like Olybrius, the emperors who followed him were all puppets of leading Germanic generals. Glycerius lasted only 15 months, followed by Julius Nepos, who made it until 475 before being deposed by his *magister militum*, Orestes, and fleeing to Dalmatia, where he remained a local ruler who still claimed the title of emperor until his assassination in 480. Back in Italy, Orestes named his teenaged son Romulus Augustulus to the throne, but he was deposed by the Hunnic ruler Odovacer on September 4, 476 and sent to the countryside. Little is known about him except that after his departure, no one bothered proclaiming an emperor of the Western Empire anymore, simply because there was nothing that could be called a Western Empire.

The overthrow of Romulus Augustulus only made explicit a state of affairs that had been in existence for more than a generation and had been in development for more than a century. In fact, the scholar Averil

Cameron called his overthrow "one of the most famous non-events in history." Due to the continuing instability, all emperors after Honorius had made Ravenna their home right until Romulus Augustulus was deposed, and Ravenna continued in importance as the capital of Ostrogothic Italy and later the Byzantine Exarchate. Its strong defenses also guaranteed that it wasn't sacked, so many of its early Christian churches are still wonderfully preserved to this day.

The Catholic Church played an increasingly important role throughout this period. While emperors were politically and militarily weak, they were still wealthy and sponsored a great deal of building of churches and monasteries. So did the wealthy elite, some of whom went as far as to take literally the injunction of Matthew 19:21: "Jesus said unto him, If thou wilt be perfect, go and sell that thou hast, and give to the poor, and thou shalt have treasure in heaven: and come and follow me." There were several examples of rich people, such as the Roman matron Marcella (who died during the sack of Rome), giving up all their estates to the Church and retiring to live lives of prayer and contemplation.

In the wake of the Western half of the Roman Empire,

Europe witnessed the development of the Middle Ages. The Church was able to weather the collapse of the Western Roman Empire thanks to the Germanic tribes being Christian themselves, and the Church's usefulness as a steadying force was also maintained. The landed gentry were also left more or less alone, because whatever ruler was in power needed them to keep the crops coming in. The Germanic people even kept much of the bureaucracy in place since they themselves didn't have the experience of running an urbanized society. As various Germanic tribes settled down - the Visigoths in the Iberian peninsula, the Franks in France, the Anglo-Saxons in England, etc. - they coalesced into small kingdoms where the king was only one force who had to share his power with the nobility and the clergy.

The face of Europe had changed. The old Roman Empire was gone in the West, and while it would survive in a changed form as the Byzantine Empire based in Constantinople until 1453, the West was already developing into a series of separate states that would dominate the Middle Ages.

# Reunification Efforts

**A contemporary mosaic depicting Justinian I**

Born as *Petrus Sabbatius*, the future Byzantine Emperor Justinian I came from a Romanized Illyrian family. There is still an ongoing dispute over the location of his birth, as he later on built a marvelous city called Iustiniana Prima near the small village where he was born. He slowly rose from the army ranks and, due to the favor of his uncle, became an Emperor of the Eastern Empire after his uncle's death.

Justinian married the actress Theodora not long before his coronation, even though she was described as a woman of loose morals and diabolical character. Still, she was the perfect match for Justinian in regard to their political and religious inclinations. She was his closest political advisor until her death in 548. There were claims that she was also a co-ruler in addition to being a Roman *augusta* and royal consort, though such claims were never proven.[10]

The Emperor Justinian inherited a strong state and a solid military system refashioned with Anastasius' army reforms from his predecessors. This was also the time of the great Avar raids, as they came from their homeland in Central Asia in several successive waves and established a mighty tribal federation in the territory known today as the Hungarian Plain. A large percentage of the people of that tribal federation were

---

[10] See Fine, 1991: 22 and the entries on Justinian and Theodora, at the Online Encyclopedia of Roman Emperors http://www.luc.edu/roman-emperors/justinia.htm and http://www.luc.edu/roman-emperors/dora.htm.

of Slavic origin. Though he had to defend the Danube lines and the Balkan provinces against raids by the Avars and Slavs, new barbarian groups which emerged in the sixth century, Justinian sent his most loyal and brilliant general, Belisarius, to reconquer Italy for him. He saw Theodoric's Ostrogoth kingdom as the main obstacle to the restitution of the Roman Empire.[11] Justinian fought for the Balkans, Italy, and North Africa for 40 years.

Justinian's endeavors were best recorded in the writings of Procopius, who was as notorious an author as Justinian was a notorious ruler. His works should always be taken with a grain of salt, as he represents the same people in utterly discrepant manners. If one takes into consideration that Procopius belonged to a senatorial order which was slowly losing its footing in the new society that Justinian and Theodora were creating, then the vitriol can be understood, while sugarcoating the same events and people can be observed as a way to hold on to the little power and influence that the senatorial class still had in Constantinople.

---
[11] Whitby, 1988:70-71.

Despite of all these shortcomings, the writings of Procopius were of great value in the history of the Ostrogoths because Procopius, as did many learned persons of the time,[12] served as scribe for a Byzantine Master of Soldiers, in his case Belisarius. During the time spent campaigning with Belisarius and his army, Procopius got firsthand information on the events he describes in his writings. He spent the period 534-540 with Belisarius in Ostrogoth Italy, and he later spent two years on the Persian front. From 542 until his death in 556, he lived in Constantinople working on his accounts.

---

[12] Compare with Jordanes, pages 2-3

**A contemporary mosaic believed to depict Belisarius**

The first of Procopius' writings was dedicated to the wars he participated in as a scribe to Belisarius. *De bellis* (also known as *Wars*) was written in 8 books.

The first and second one covered the Persian Wars, the third and the fourth described the Vandal Wars and the fifth, sixth and seventh books were dedicated to the Goth Wars. The final volume was a miscellaneous addition to the previous seven books. The first seven books were published at the end of 550 or the beginning of 551, while the last one was published in 553.[13] The books dedicated to the Goth Wars were the most informative because they provided excurses on the everyday life and social order of the Goths. The source of these accounts was both his direct contact with the people in question and his understanding of older written accounts.

After finishing *De bellis*, Procopius dedicated his time on writing the *Historia arcana* (*The Secret History*). In this work, the previously coherent, learned and experienced military observer gave place to the bitter, open critic of Justinian, his consort Theodora, Belisarius and many other Court members. If one can see beyond the highly colored gossip and senatorial snobbery, this data is a useful addition to the information provided in the *Wars,* as it gives a better representation of the events that lead to the reconquest

---
[13] Barišić *et al.* 1995: 25

of Italy.[14]

According to Procopius, the task to take back Italy from the Ostrogoths was given to General Belisarius. A rather convenient excuse for the realization of such intentions was provided by the death of the pro-Byzantine Ostrogoth queen Amalasuntha by the hands of her cousin and co-ruler Theodahad. The first attack on Theodahad and Italy was made in 535, when the armies lead by the Master of Soldiers Belisarius invaded Italy and made their way to modern-day Palermo. Theodahad was killed by his own people because of this military failure and the Ostrogoth Witigis was instituted as the new Ostrogoth king in 536. The short reign of Witigis marked the last attempt of the Ostrogoths to preserve the integrity of their Italian kingdom.

Witigis left for Ravenna after leaving a small force to guard Rome. While in Ravenna, he married Theodoric's granddaughter, Matasuntha, against her will, in order to reinforce his claims to the throne via marriage to a princess of the older dynasty. While Witigis was concentrating his forces in Ravenna, the

---

[14] *Ibidem*, 31

Pope Silverius surrendered Rome to General Belisarius. Witigis retaliated in 537 with a siege on Rome and tried to cut the water supply to Belisarius' armies. Damaging the Roman aqueducts proved to be a bad move, as the water flooded Witigis' camp and turned it into a malaria infested swamp.

This military failure was followed by a three-month truce, but the Byzantine general broke the treaty by attacking Picenum. A year later, in the spring of 538, the Goths gave up on the siege of Rome. Their power was still felt in Northern Italy for two more years, despite the fact that the only haven they had was Ravenna. Ultimately, Witigis saw the solution to this military conundrum in his own abdication, after which his noblemen offered his throne to Belisarius. While giving the false illusion that he was accepting the throne as a ruler of the Ostrogoths, Belisarius entered Ravenna, after which he took Witigis and his unwilling wife Matasuntha, many on their noble retinue and what has left of Theodoric's treasure to Constantinople.[15]

The brilliant Master of Soldiers Belisarius finally got a worthy opponent in the newly appointed Ostrogoth king

---

[15] http://www.britannica.com/EBchecked/topic/646154/Witigis.

Totila, who ruled in the Kingdom of Italy from his ascension in the autumn of 541 until his death in 552. Totila was chosen to rule after Witigis and his retinue were taken as captives in Constantinople, but Totila proved to be quite the obstacle to Justinian's plans for uniting the old empires. By 543, through fighting on sea and land, Totila and his armies had reconquered much of Italy, but the Eternal City was holding its own and refused to surrender, despite Totila's address to the Senate demanding obedience in the name of Theodoric, to whom Rome owed alliance.

**Illustration depicting Totila attacking Florence**

Justinian retaliated by sending Belisarius on yet another military campaign against the Goths, but in 545, Totila began a massive siege of Rome, enabled by the enlargement of his ranks with escaped Roman slaves and captives of the previous battles. Belisarius decided to try to feed the besieged city in secret instead of engaging in open battle, where he would have been outnumbered and out-resourced.[16] Nonetheless, by 546, the starved Eternal City surrendered to the hands of the Ostrogoth king. Totila showed mercy to them by not letting his soldiers violate the female population and by sending more and more food every day.

After seizing the city, Totila sent ambassadors to Justinian saying that he wished to discontinue the war and wanted to make the same arrangement with them that Theodoric had with the older Byzantine Emperors: to rule in Italy with Justinian as his overlord and to owe his alliance, armies, and taxes to Byzantium. Yet, he said that if refused, he would tear the walls of Rome to the ground and start launching raids on Illyricum.[17]

The battles between Constantinople and Totila continued off and on until the end of 550, but in 551, another of Justinian's generals, the eunuch named Narses, dealt the final blow to Totila's resistance. While Belisarius was waging war on Italy and Persia prior to 550, Narses had been dealing with the problems arising on the Danube frontiers, but Justinian sent Narses with an army of 30,000 soldiers to Italy after that. It took a year to reconquer Tiginae in the Apennines, and Totila

---
[16] http://www.britannica.com/EBchecked/topic/600536/Totila.
[17] Bury, 1923: 244-245.

was mortally injured in this battle and succumbed to his wounds shortly after. Narses fought the Ostrogoths and crushed their resistance in two more years, and he also was able to fend off raids by the Franks, who tried to take advantage of the unrest in Northern Italy.

Narses was well respected by Justinian for his military successes, but not by his successor, Justin II, who stripped Narses of all his military honors and exiled him to Naples. As for the Ostrogoths, one of their generals named Teia was elected king after the devastating battle of Tiginae, but he did not live long enough to rule. Narses' armies killed him in the battle near Mons Lactarius at the end of 552 or beginning of 553,[18] marking the end of the Ostrogoth resistance in Italy before it reverted completely to Byzantine control.

As for Justinian's great schemes for uniting both halves of the once great Roman Empire, things did not turn out as planned. Though he had conquered Italy, Northern Africa, and the greater portion of Gaul with the help of Belisarius and Narses, he decimated both his royal coffers and his armies in doing so. His constant war against the nations he perceived as obstacles for his

---
[18] *Ibidem,* 250.

plans demanded a constant influx of soldiers, and he had supplemented his ranks by retrieving troops from the Danube *limitanei* stations and leaving the northern frontier vulnerable to attacks by the Avars and Slavs. The increased taxes he imposed on the local population, who retaliated by fleeing and joining the barbarian troops instead of cultivating the land, made things even worse.

In the end, the attempt to reunite the empires was probably a futile task if only because the religious and cultural divisions that had come into existence long before were too great to be filled with an administrative merger. Shortly after Justinian's death in 565, a very demanding war started between the Persians and the weakened Danube lines, which offered almost no protection against the Avar-Slavic raids (by this time an almost annual matter).[19] All things considered, the annihilation of the Ostrogoth kingdom was a Pyrrhic victory for Justinian, although the Exarchate of Ravenna, a Byzantine establishment, took the place of the Ostrogoth kingdom of Italy until its fall in 751 to raids by the Lombards.

---

[19] Fine, 1991:24

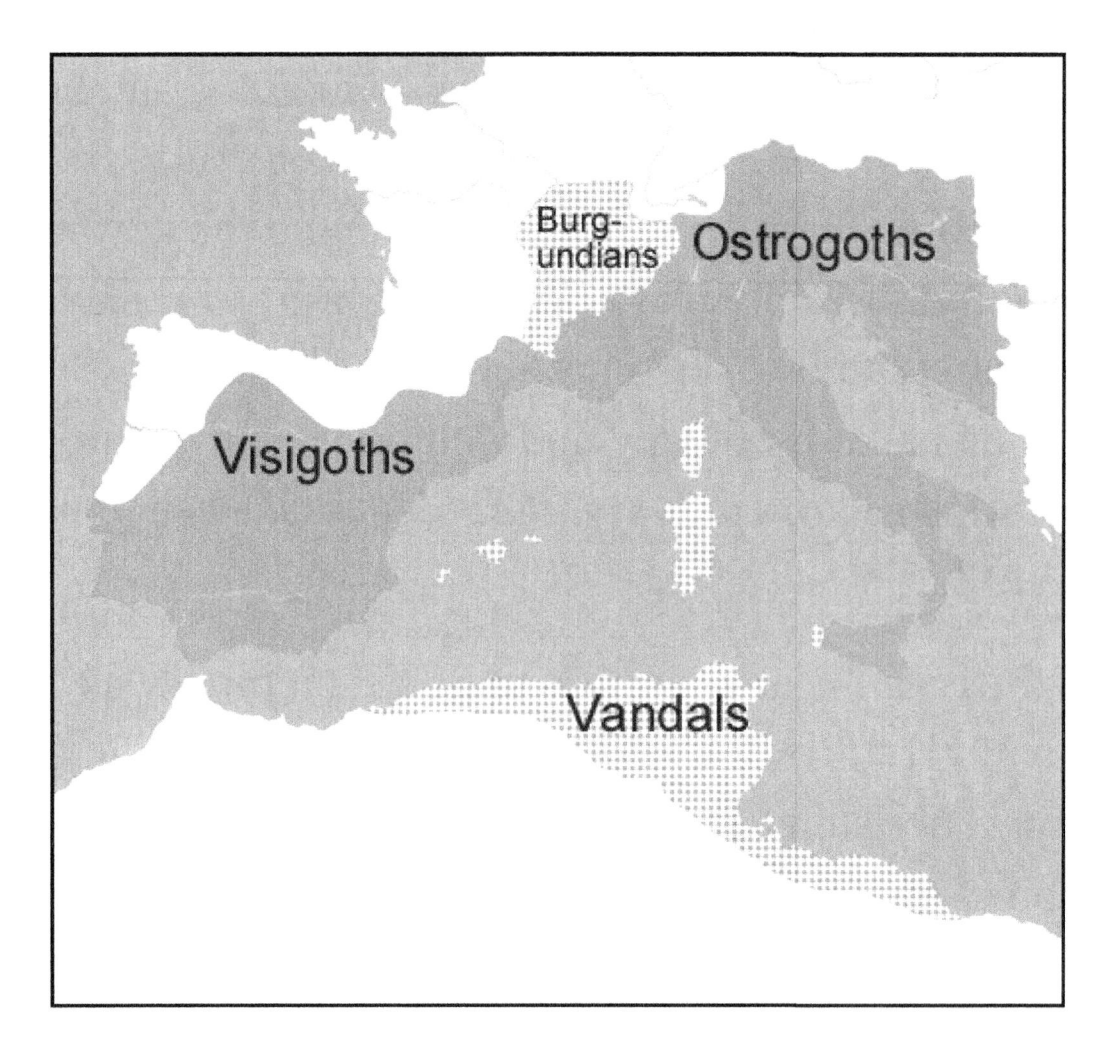

**The extent of Gothic possessions in the early 6th century**

Though it's often forgotten today, Ravenna, now a Northern Italian city in Emilia Romagna, was both the capital of the Western Roman Empire and the Ostrogoth Kingdom of Italy. Honorius, the first Emperor of the Western Empire, had moved the capital from Rome to Ravenna, a port city on the delta along the river Po and the Adriatic Sea.[20] His half-sister, Gala Placidia, first the wife of a Goth king and later of a Roman Emperor, was buried in Ravenna, and Odoacer made his see in Ravenna and ruled for 11 years before the arrival of Theodoric and the creation of his kingdom. Ravenna thrived under the patronage on Theodoric, who restored and rebuilt a palace for himself, as well as several churches. All these structures still shine with the same splendor today as the day they were built, and Theodoric was buried near one of the churches he built, San Apollinare Nuovo, in a rotund mausoleum.

**A mosaic depicting Theodoric the Great's palace**

---

[20] Cirelli, 2010:241

## chapel at San Apollinare Nuovo.

Along with the political and military influence befitting a capital, Ravenna was one of the most important religious centers in Late Antiquity. Some of its ecclesiastical edifices were built by Theodoric and praise the Arian version of Christianity, while others were built or renovated to prove the Byzantine supremacy over the city and the Ostrogoth kingdom. Adding to all of this was the fact that the excellent strategic position and the nearby port made Ravenna the main trade point between the Eastern and the Western Empire.[21]

The Empress Galla Placidia was a well-known patron of arts. Under her patronage, churches dedicated to St. John the Baptist and Santa Maria Maggiore were built. She also commissioned the building of the Church of the Holy Cross, to which a small building was adjoined. This building might have served as an oratorio for the church, but it is also believed to be the Mausoleum of Galla Placidia. It is unknown if one of the three sarcophagi contains her remains, as the Basilica of St. Peter at Rome was used as a mausoleum for the

---
[21] Lowden, 1997:104.

Theodosian family, but in any event, the exterior of the mausoleum is simple brickwork done in a cross-shaped form. The interior is covered with a multitude of mosaics done in rich gold, blue and green. Each of the cross' arms is covered with a vault decorated with mosaics and features lunettes (semi-circular walls where a vault ends.)

One of the lunettes features the most famous mosaic scene of the Mausoleum: *The Good Shepard,* showing a young, king-like Jesus, garbed in royal colors, tending to his flock while sitting on a rock. The second lunette contains an interesting scene depicting St. Lawrence as he prepared to sacrifice himself in blazing fires for the Christian faith. His strong belief is symbolized by a large crucifix on his shoulders and a cabinet filled with scrolls of the Gospels. The mosaics are bordered with depictions of floral motifs in the most opulent blues and greens. The ceilings of the vaults are decorated with intricate rosettes on a midnight blue backdrop. It is truly a resting place worthy of a Roman Empress and a wife of a Goth king.[22]

Theodoric was believed to have built a great palace for

---
[22] Bovini, 1991: 12-24.

himself, but the place and the exact configuration of the palace is still a subject for debate because the archaeological remains of the so-called Theodoric's palace dated to a late period. Today, only the niched façade of the edifice is still standing.[23]

Nonetheless, the mosaics that graced the walls and domes of many of the churches of Ravenna tell the story of a city that is no more. The church of San Apollinaire Nuovo is decorated with a mosaic in the upper region of the southern interior wall depicting the palace of Theodoric, and based on what can still be seen, it appears to have been an elegant, several storied edifice of slender, white columns, with a lush interior. What is left intact of this palace is the palatial church of San Apollinaire Nuovo[24]. This church was built by Theodoric in 504, shortly after the arrival of the Ostrogoths in Italy, though the dedication to Saint Apollinare did not happen until the middle of the 9th century after the relics of the saint were moved from the nearby church of San Apollinare in Classe, a nearby port. At that time, they were in danger due to the constant raids from the Adriatic Sea. The church was

---
[23] *Ibidem*, 82
[24] Vercone, 1968:95-96

subsequently renamed "the New Church of Saint Apollinaire."

When he was alive, Theodoric dedicated this church to Christ the Redeemer. According to the *Liber Pontificalis Ecclesiae Ravennatis*, a donor's inscription with the text in Latin in the apse claimed, "King Theodoric built this church from its foundations in the name of Our Lord Jesus Christ."[25] Justinian introduced great changes to its interior and rededicated it to Saint Martin of Tours, a 4$^{th}$ century bishop who was a formidable opponent of Arianism.

As for the architecture of the church, it is a monumental three nave basilica. The whole interior was decorated with mosaic images, and of the original mosaics done in the time of Theodoric, 26 panels represented scenes from the life and passion of Christ, as well as Theodoric's palace and the *Classe* port. They now decorate the nave of the Church, done in bold pastel colors on a golden backdrop.

This church bears the signs of the political struggle that was ongoing in Ravenna during the second half of the Sixth Century, but not in the form of blunt

---
[25] Bovini, 1991:59.

destruction as much as in a *damnatio memoriae* fashion. After the refurnishing of 651, mosaic images of saints, angels, and martyrs were added and older mosaic details were deleted. The palace and the port were probably decorated with depictions of Theodoric and his royal family accompanied by their retinue, but Justinian's restoration removed these images, and blackened space between the curtains was added. Still, the rendering of masonry is the main motif in the port scene. Furthermore, a small detail, either left on purpose by a sympathetic artisan or simply a negligent mistake, speaks louder than all this banishing; a small hand protruding from a richly embroidered sleeve is still visible against one of the columns, as if it was waving a secret greeting to the Gothic king who altered the city's history forever.[26]

  Another important building commissioned by Theodoric at the same time as the church of Saint Apollinaire was the Arian Baptistery. He wanted to give his people, all of them devoted to Arianism, a church reflecting their particular Christian beliefs, and he dedicated it to the Resurrection. In 561, the church was re-dedicated to St. Theodore after the fall of the

___

[26] *Ibidem*: 60-65

Ostrogoth kingdom. The Baptistery is called "Arian" today so as to distinguish it from the other nearby baptistery built by Bishops Ursus and Neon a century earlier. Today, this edifice is called the Neonian Baptistery, or the Orthodox one.

The Arian Baptistery was an octagonal building, its interior filled with niches depicting scenes from the baptism of Christ. The central dome scene showed Jesus as a pre-pubescent young man being baptized by John the Baptist, who was easily distinguished by his clothing made of animal skins, the uniform of the desert ascetic. A bearded, elderly person with a long, white beard holding an amphora observed the scene, a personification of the river Jordan. The lower section depicts a procession of apostles, each half led by St. Peter and St. Paul to bow in front of a jeweled *codex* of the Bible laid out on a lush purple cushion. Though the images were almost a carbon copy of the ones from the older Neonian Baptistery and nothing heretic was present, after 565 the baptistery was converted into an oratory for the nearby monastery of St. Mary of Cosmedin. The mosaics remained intact, still vividly representing the descent of the Holy Spirit, in the form of a white dove, on top of the half-submerged young

Jesus.[27]

One of Theodoric's great legacies was his final resting place, the Mausoleum built near the city's center. It is still located among a small forest of cypress trees known as "Campo Cordeiro." This was a sacred burial ground used by the Goths, as shown by the archaeological excavations undertaken in the 20th and 21st centuries. The writings of a scholar who was almost a contemporary of Theodoric, known under the name of *Anonymous Valesii*, inform us that the great king built himself 'a monument of great squared rocks.' Indeed, the rotund, two-story building was built of stone imported from the nearby town of Istria with a rough-hewn, decagonal structure also erected. The upper story was also decagonal on the outside and a bit smaller than the lower section, while the interior was completely circular. The roof was made of a great monolith core, also imported from Istria. As for the structure left unfinished, many discussions exist on what should have been its final form. The upper story holds a porphyry coffin that might have been used as a bath tub before its employment as a sarcophagus, a practice not unknown in the rest of Byzantium. The coffin was found empty,

[27] *Ibidem*, 51-52.

which raises the possibility that burial happened at some other location or that the body was moved postmortem.[28]

Rebuilding the churches built as a commission from Theodoric was not enough for the Byzantine Emperor Justinian, who wanted as many visible proofs as possible that Italy was his again. The Byzantine bishop Maximianus was sent to Ravenna in 546 to restore the proper faith and oversee the building of two churches which reflected the Imperial benevolence on the city. Though the building of these churches was not publicly funded by the Imperial pair, they did send gifts and probably skilled artisans from the Capitol, to add to its lavishness. The patron who funded the projects was a local merchant by the name Julianus, also called Argentarius ("the banker.") It is recorded that the building of St. Vitale cost 26,000 golden solidi.[29] Except for the fact that he was an avid supporter of the arts and a person of many funds, history give little information about Argentarius.

The Basilica of St. Vitale is easily one of the most magnificent churches of Christendom. Architecturally,

---
[28] Bovini, 1991:120-124.
[29] *Ibidem*, 25.

it is not an elongated basilica typical for the Western Empire, but it has an octagonal form topped with a large dome and a rectangular presbytery with an apse. The lushness of the church comes from its rotund form and the play of the well-focused light on the jewel-colored mosaics. Just as with the other churches with mosaic decorations from Ravenna, the main theme was the life and passion of Christ. However, Old Testament scenes like that of Abraham showing hospitality to the three angels did make an appearance.[30]

Two mosaics render this church different from its contemporaries, one mosaic panel depicting Justinian with his retinue and another of his wife Theodora accompanied by her ladies in waiting. It was not uncommon for the donors and the ruling families to have their images immortalized in the edifices they built in Byzantium. On the contrary, it was quite the practice. Here, the portraits of Justinian and Theodora symbolized the Byzantine supremacy over the Ostrogoths and the Arian heresy. If one takes into consideration a newer theory that the building of both St. Vitale and St. Apollinaire in Classe began before the arrival of Maximianus in Ravenna, it is quite possible

---
[30] Lowden, 1997: 79.

that Argentarius was just a "smokescreen" for Justinian's actions during a time when Ravenna was still Ostrogoth. He might even have sent funds to help finish the building projects. Another opinion is that this scene is an invocation of an older, real-life occasion of the Imperial couple bearing lavishly decorated liturgical tools as gifts to the Hagia Sophia Church, located in the Capitol and also built under the tutelage of Justinian.[31]

  The two mosaic panels representing the Imperial couple were on the side walls of the apse, which is decorated with an image of St. Vitalis, the patron saint of the church, receiving his martyr crown from a seated, youthful looking Jesus. The representation of Justinian is on the north wall. The Emperor, garbed in a royal gold and purple mantle and wearing a heavily jeweled crown is accompanied by two deacons and a bishop holding a cross, identified as Maximianus by a short inscription over his head. One of the deacons carried a jeweled Bible, the other a censer. The Emperor himself is represented holding a golden vessel known as a paten and is accompanied with three other noblemen and a small troop of soldiers, their shields decorated with Christ's monogram (the "chi-ro" symbol.) The objects

---
[31] Bovini, 1991:26.

that Justinian and his retinue carry were to be used in liturgy and most probably their real counterparts were sent as gifts for the newly consecrated church. Theodora is represented holding a jeweled chalice while standing next to a fountain, with one of the noblemen raising a curtain so she could enter.[32] The flamboyant woman described by Procopius cannot be seen; instead, a solemn and regal lady stands in front of the viewer. Her ladies-in-waiting were also depicted in rich, colorful clothing. Theodora's mantle even had a depiction of the Adoration of the Magi, as if to point out further the imperial attention to bearing gifts.

The Church of Saint Apollinaire in Classe was built at the same time and also funded by Argentarius and consecrated by Bishop Maximianus. Unlike St. Vitale, this church had the standard form of an elongated basilica, where the mosaic decoration was focused on the nave (completely preserved) and the floor (of which only a small section near the left and right aisle remains.) Once the lower sections of the church were richly inlaid with marble, but this was removed in the 15th century and set aside to be used in a church in the nearby town of Rimini. Of the original marble work,

---
[32] Lowden, 1997: 80.

the slender columns made of imported Proconnesian marble were intact. Also a very opulent church, even if it lacks the St. Vitale richness of mosaics, its building might have served to stress even further the Byzantine presence in the city. The long, thin line of red bricks on the exterior marks it as Justinian's church, because the same can be seen in every ecclesiastical project he sponsored or approved. Its location is not coincidental, because he who held the port held the city as well. Today, due to the shifting of the shoreline, the church is about three miles away from the sea, though once it was located on the very seaside.

The relics of St. Apollinaire, the first bishop of Ravenna and presumed to have been a disciple of St. Peter, were used for the consecration of the church. Later on, due to danger, they were moved to St. Apollinare Nuevo (the new church of St. Apollinaire) and thus gave its new name to the church that was actually older than the Classe church.

Ultimately, the Goths traveled a long way from the frozen Scandinavian lands to the marshes of Ukraine. Along the way, they separated into two different groups, but they still shared similar cultures and beliefs, and both groups made profound (albeit different) impacts on European history. Both the Ostrogoth and Visigoth people contributed their fair share to the events shaping the history of the Balkan lands before each of the groups left for Italy and Gaul respectively.

The barbarians of the Early Middle Ages are often seen by modern historians as a cause of destruction instead of a force of positive change, and this belief was brought about in part because of ancient historians who were biased by their own viewpoints. That said, some writers did the Goths justice by describing them as loyal, sturdy soldiers and mentioning that their rulers did not exact violence and destruction if it wasn't necessary. In the writings of Procopius, Totila and Theodoric were juxtaposed as fair, levelheaded rulers, especially in comparison to Justinian.

If there was ever a barbarian nation that was the extreme opposite of the savage barbarian stereotype, it was the Ostrogoth nation. They certainly dealt serious damage to both the Eastern and Western Empires, as well as any other nation that compelled the Ostrogoths to fight for a realm of their own, but this was inevitable. From the 3rd-7th centuries, Europe was a great melting pot of new people, new religions, new cultures and new ways of waging war. This added up to an explosive atmosphere where even the smallest action by one group could set off a butterfly effect that led to great changes elsewhere.

The removal of the Ostrogoths ended the danger they represented to the integrity of the Balkan provinces, but it proved to be a short-lived remedy. The Ostrogoth Kingdom of Italy was a prosperous enterprise under the Arian ruler Theodoric, with tolerance for the people belonging to different religions and religious factions, as well as people with different backgrounds and social status. However, all that ended due Justinian's ambitions to unite the Western and Eastern Empire into one. After 40 years of waging wars, the territory was claimed back from the various barbarian people who had settled there, but the Byzantines themselves had no funds left to govern Italy or rebuild their depleted armies.

Nonetheless, the Ostrogoth legacy in Northern Italy is abundant and plentiful, ranging from archaeological sites where the artifacts tell the stories of the everyday life and social structure to masterful churches built by those of the Arian faith. Though many of these edifices bear the traces of *"damnatio memoriae,"* they still speak of the great architectural genius and highly developed artistic spirit of their builders. These monuments are the most valuable legacy left by the great Goth nation, not the battles they won or the territories they claimed.

As for the Byzantines, who referred to their empire as the Roman Empire for centuries, they would struggle to maintain their grip on power in the region, culminating with the Ottoman siege of Constantinople in 1453.

## The Rise of the Ottomans

The origins of the Ottoman Empire and the dynasty that founded it are surrounded by legends and mysteries. The mythology around Osman I and his closest family created an image of the dynasty, legitimizing their heritage and right to rule. While some of it surely is true, a lot of it may also be sheer exaggeration. Even the true origin of the Ottoman dynasty is heavily debated by modern historians. The general opinion is that the Ottomans descended from the Kayi tribe, a branch of the Oghuz Turks. This was never mentioned in any records actually written by the time of Osman I's life, but firstly 200 years later, which makes it a highly contested statement. Contemporaneous writers would claim Osman to be a descendant of the Kayi tribe to aggrandize him.

The Kayi Tribe was powerful, prosperous and played an important role in the Caucasus region, both at the time before Osman was born and for hundreds of years to come. To link the Ottoman dynasty with such a tribe would work as an incentive to keep up good relations with the actual Kayi tribe, and also inflate the story about how the Ottoman dynasty descended from power and political influence. It would also support the inherited right of the Ottoman dynasty to rule the area. Though this may never be clearly settled amongst historians today, we do know that Osman's family was one of many Oghuz Turkish people originating from what today is western Kazakhstan, just east of the Caspian Sea.

From there, the Seljuk tribe of Oghuz people moved southwest into Persia and founded their empire, slowly moving west towards the Byzantine Empire. When the Seljuk Empire disintegrated, many smaller states were formed all over Anatolia and Osman's father Ertugrul was a ruler of one of them. Legend has it that Ertugrul and his army of 400 horse-borne fighters accidentally came upon a battle between two foreign armies. Heroically he decided to intervene and support the side currently losing. With his help, they turned the battle and won. Ertugrul learned that he had been fighting on the side of the Sultan of Konya, from the capital of Rum, against the invading forces of the Mongolian armies.

As a reward for his actions, he was handed a piece of land in northwestern Anatolia, centered around the town of Sögut. The truth in this story is again under debate since it wasn't written down until much later. There is no clear evidence of how Ertugrul came in possession of the lands he ruled or what his relationship was with the Sultanate of Rum. All we can say for sure is that this became the embryo of the Ottoman Empire as Ertugrul settled down, got married and later also had a son, Osman. This happened sometime in the middle of the 13th century, but the exact date of Osman's birth was never recorded.

During the years of Osman's childhood, his father was the chief of his given lands but also subordinated the

Sultanate of Rum. When Osman was 23, his father died and Osman inherited the title and power Ertugrul had earned. It was now nearing the end of the 13th century and the Sultanate of Rum, as well as the whole Seljuk Empire, was disintegrating. The rise and expansion of Osman's territory came more or less as a natural consequence, replacing one power with another. It was a gradual process going on for generations of the Ottoman dynasty and Osman's early conquerings were only a fraction of how large the empire would become. The necessity of expansion was in later years explained with the spreading of the Muslim faith. The truth behind this is a contaminated topic among modern historians and hard to verify. Islam is no longer considered to be a driving force for either Ertugrul or Osman. Ertugrul was not a Muslim, but many claim Osman's religious father-in-law converted him to the faith. The story of how Osman became a devout Muslim is of importance to the Ottoman legacy. It includes a prophecy where God himself appoints Osman and his descendants to glory and success. This was in later centuries used to legitimize the continued rule of his heirs. It was also Osman who named the whole empire and the following dynasty, still alive today. Osman is the Arabic version of the Turkish Uthman, or Athman, which scholars believe was Osman's real name. His name changed into Osman under influence from the Arabic and Persian Islamic culture, to signal his transcendence into a Muslim. Whether or not Osman was religious he decided to expand into Byzantine territory and kept peace with his Turkish neighbors. Until the actual dissolution of the Seljuk Empire, the Ottoman dynasty did not fight other Turkish tribes.

To try to pinpoint the descent and origins of the Ottoman dynasty and Osman himself is more or less impossible today. The sources are highly contaminated with propaganda like factoids about Osman's persona, his heroic actions and the constant success of his ambitions, written at the height of the Ottoman Empire hundreds of years after Osman's reign. There are hardly any actual records from his childhood and we know very little about his early years of conquest. Probably because at the time being, Osman's father and family were not considered particularly mighty or influential. Thus, the lack of contemporaneous writings implies the falsehood of the anachronistic records speaking of Osman's visions and also of his father's heroic intervention against the Mongol army. Anatolia consisted of many beyliks at the time, as well as different alliances between tribes from all over Eurasia, Eastern Europe, Middle East and as far away as Central Asia. The number of interconnections and movements between the different tribes are uncountable, which makes it harder to factually pin down the true origins of Osman's ancestors. Whoever the ascendants of Osman truly were one can safely say that his descendants, using his very name, would be well-known to historians and civilians for many centuries.

As stated above, Osman was born as the son of a chief in northwestern Anatolia, in the town of Söguk sometime around the middle of the 13th century. The exact year has not been confirmed by any reliable sources, but 1258 is usually mentioned as most likely. His mother is presumed to be Halime Hatun, but even this has not been securely confirmed, and hardly anything is recorded of who she was. We know safely that Osman grew up in his hometown with two brothers but until his marriage to Mal Hatun there's not much information of his whereabouts. As the firstborn son of a local chief, Osman was aware of the fact that he would someday inherit the position, and it is said he learned to ride and fight already as a child. The first story recorded by the 15th-century historians of the Ottoman Empire is the one about how Osman became a Muslim. It was during a visit at his good friend Sheik Edebali's house, who was a very religious man, that he found the Quran. Osman became interested and asked his friend what this book was. His friend, who was an influential religious man in the community told him it was the holy book of Islam.

Osman lay awake that night, reading and reading until he couldn't keep his eyes open anymore. He fell asleep at the auspicious hour of dawn and then dreamed of a tree, sprouting from his navel with branches reaching all over the world. People in the dream were happy and the landscape was beautiful. When he woke up in the morning he told Edebali about the strange dream who in turn explained that because Osman had read the book so intensely and honestly, God had chosen him and his descendants to be blessed with glory and honor for many generations to come. Sheikh Edebali then gladly gave Osman his daughter Mal Sultana to marry and of their love, many poems have been written. The union of the two families benefited Osman greatly according to later sources because Sheikh Edebali was associated with very devout and ascetic dervishes. Though the dervishes didn't have any riches or power, their relationship to Allah would help benefit the Ottoman dynasty. The story of how Osman was the first in the family to actually become a devout Muslim was important to legitimize him taking over the remnants of the Seljuk Empire.

Osman's dream wasn't written down until almost 200 years later, a time when such a story would be of importance to keep the Ottoman Empire united. The story was valuable to the unification of separate Muslim emirates and gave Osman the right to conquer them. Another tradition that bears Osman's name is the girding of the sword of Islam given to him by his father-in-law. Every sultan of the Ottoman Empire was girt with a ceremonial sword within two weeks of their accession to the throne, although not the same sword as Osman received from Edebali. Again, this practice was only introduced when Islam already had emerged as the prevalent ideology of the Ottoman Empire long after Osman's death, and again, the ceremony was mainly used to inflate the religious importance of the dynasty.

The year after his marriage to Mal Sultana, which probably took room in 1280, Osman's father passed away and left the 23-year-old son in charge of the beylik. The timing was perfect for Osman to become a world-famous conqueror and founder of an empire. In the west, the Byzantine Empire was falling apart and many cities made easy targets for Osman's army. In the east, the Mongols were wreaking havoc, contributing to the decline of the Seljuk Empire, and forced many Turks to flee the territories under Mongol siege. A great many ghazi warriors and potential soldiers streamed into Osman's emirate and gladly joined him in his quest against the Byzantine Empire.

The tradition of Ghazi warriors has been compared with the idea of the crusades or jihad. The word means "to carry out a military expedition or raid" in Arabic, but some scholars also mean that it indicates that the ghazi warrior fought to spread Islam. This is another fact debated in modern research, and there are no contemporaneous sources confirming that Osman was fighting in the name of Islam or that he really was a devout Muslim. As stated, these implications were written down much later by religious history writers at a time when they wanted to portray the founder of the empire as God's chosen man. What is known about the ghazi warriors is that they most likely fought as mercenaries and hence changed sides to whoever could pay them at the moment. Whatever their reasons might have been, the ghazi warriors were important contributors to Osman's success. Osman also added the word ghazi to his name, as did eight of his successors. Whether all of them defined themselves as simply conquerors or as religious men, it is impossible to say. The adding of Ghazi to their name nonetheless indicated their expansionist intentions.

  After Osman had gotten married and his father had passed away, he was a full-fledged leader of the beylik, with a strategically important territory and prosperous family ties through his marriage. The stream of warriors and refugees made Osman a ruler of more people than his father, and with more people, more lands were needed. To expand at the cost of the Byzantine Empire was a logical solution, and it is estimated that he started his expansionist campaign in the year 1288. His first target was two nearby fortresses, Karacahisar and Eskişehir. A decade later, in 1299, he conquered the two larger towns of Yarhisar and Bilecik from the crumbling Byzantine Empire. He made Yarhisar the new capital of the beylik and declared independence from the Seljuk Empire.

By then, the central rule of the empire was weak and the popular sultan had been forced to flee the lands a couple of decades earlier. In his wake, there was chaos and no strong ruling power. The newly born independent state under Osman was organized as a strong central government on the same principles as the previous Sultanate of Rum. Though many people in the peripheries were opposed to Osman's rule, he quickly lightened the tax burden of his new citizens which assuaged them and changed the negative opinion of him. He needed to establish trust and loyalty amongst the people who are furthest from the capital to stabilize the borders, and the low tax strategy worked well. He was also the first chief in the area to mint his own coins which points to Osman's ambition of creating a larger organized political entity.

After the declaration of independence, Osman continued to expand both southwest and north into Byzantine territory aiming to control the whole area between the Sea of Marmara and the Black Sea. He conquered towns along the coasts and the poorly organized Byzantine armies were coerced to draw back towards the Bosphorus. In 1308 he captured the last city on the Aegean coast, Ephesus, and thus achieved his goals of dominating the region. His mounted forces used multiple creative military strategies for defeating the enemies around the countryside of Bithynia and fought in ever-surprising formations. During his last years in life, he also had good help from his sons, especially the oldest, the heir to the throne Orhan. After a whole life on the battlefields with his father, Orhan had learned and fully mastered the ideas behind Osman's tactics.

The last successful campaign of Osman was the siege of Bursa, though his son was left in charge and Osman himself didn't participate physically. Orhan showed tenacity and chose to lay siege to the city instead of attacking and conquer it forcefully. The siege was successful and the city surrendered after two of years under the threat of starvation. This was the last and most important victory of Osman I's expansion in Anatolia, not fully complete until the same year Osman died, 1326. After Bursa fell under Ottoman rule, other cities in the vicinity soon followed suit. It became the new capital under Orhan and an important staging ground against further expansion to the west.

It is difficult to separate the legends surrounding Osman from facts, and little is known about his earliest endeavors. Osman gained some interest from contemporaneous writers with the capture of Ephesus and that's the first time he is mentioned in historical records from his own time. From 1308 there are reliable sources about how and what he managed to achieve, and the second half of his life is less mysterious than the first half. Osman's conquests gained importance because his son and grandson continued his expansionist ambitions and at the same time incorporated religious tolerance and political stability in their rule. No one could at the time was able to foresee what the Ottoman Empire would grow to be, though people already in an early stage took refuge under Osman and preferred him to many other rulers. When the Seljuk Empire finally disintegrated and collapsed in 1308 Osman's prosperous lands was a capacious, natural escape from raiding Mongols. After his death at the age of 68 his son, Orhan continued the expansion far beyond what his father had dreamed.

**A picture of the tomb of Osman**

By the time of Osman's death and Orhan's ascension to the throne, there are more reliable sources, to be found. It's possible to retell certain historical dates and happenings correctly but still, Orhan's reign is also somewhat glorified and exaggerated by the history writers. Orhan was probably born in the year 1281, as the only son to Osman I and his first wife, Malhun Hatun. Before Orhan conquered Bursa in 1326 not much is known of him. He was over 40 years old when Osman died and left him in command of the territories he had conquered, all of which he, together with his brother Alaeddin took good care of. Alaeddin was the second son of Osman, but born of his second wife Rabia Bala Hatun, a woman of Arabic descent. There are still some divisive opinions about which of the two brothers actually were the oldest, but their different personalities are usually seen as a natural explanation for their partition of duties. Orhan became the chief as appointed by their father and later he made Alaeddin the vizier. Orhan was a military man, who had spent much of his adult life campaigning throughout Anatolia with Osman while Alaeddin was calm, benevolent, pious and more passive, and had received management training in administration and business.

  The affinity between them stands out as something of an oddity in the Ottoman family. As the empire grew so did also the hunger for power, and the brothers of succeeding generations fought hard to claim the throne. In later years, the death of a sultan was cause for civil war to break out, and having your competing brothers murdered in cold blood. Alaeddin and Orhan, on the other hand, shared the duties and collaborated to rule the beylik even though Orhan was the one officially sitting on the throne. The story of how the brothers decided to share the burden is more or less fabricated to shine a glorifying light on them. The noble Orhan offered the throne to his brother, who, just as noble, turned it down stating their father had wanted Orhan as his heir. Orhan asked Alaeddin to become his vizier, a title he invented there and which simply means "bearer of a burden." This indicates that the brothers felt the inherited burden of responsibility from their father's accomplishments. Alaeddin accepted the title and only asked for a small patch of land close to Bursa while Orhan kept the rest of the lands under his rule. The records tell of how Orhan often sought Alaeddin's advice on administering and managing both the civil and the military institutions of the state. Together they shaped a strongly centralized government that became significant for the Ottoman Empire and modernized both politics, economy and military during its existence.

 Before Alaeddin died in 1331 or 1332, he made important contributions to Orhan's rule. In 1329 he suggested to standardize a monetary system all over the beylik, to choose an official costume or outfit for the Ottomans and to reorganize the army. Coins with Orhan's name was stamped in the same year, white became the official color of the modest clothing worn by government and military officials, and the army was divided into smaller squadrons. This initiative implies that before there probably hadn't been any similar way to organize the soldiers, though it would later become the standard. With smaller units each led by an officer it was possible applying more advanced tactics and strategies in field battles. This system is usually attributed to Alaeddin in Ottoman records, though its origins still are under debate. He also suggested forming an army which only was summoned in wartime, and hence could contribute to society in other ways during times of peace. This is largely how modern armies use their soldiers today, but the idea was new for the time. The first experiment failed under Orhan's rule, because the armies lacked military training when needed. In later generations, these armies came in very useful.

   Orhan had gotten married a first time in 1299, which resulted in two or three sons. Two of them reached fame and many sources can confirm their lives and whereabouts. Suleyman Pasha was the oldest and intended heir to the throne. He helped his father expanding his emirate mostly to the west and north taking big chunks of the Byzantine lands. After Bursa fell under Ottoman rule, the Byzantine commander chose to side with Orhan and their forces joined together. Orhan's armies kept deprecating the west and northern coastlines around the sea of Marmara and Bosporus. The Byzantine Emperor Andronicus III would not yield without a fight and was determined to stop Orhan in his advances and regain some of the lost lands.

The Battle of Pelekanon in 1329 was the first time the Byzantine armies met the Ottoman forces. The clash ended with a shattering defeat for the attacking Byzantines, although their numbers were larger and they possessed more experience from battle than the Ottomans. Contemporaneous sources explain the crushing win with the Byzantine spirit already being broken by the empire's civil struggles while the confidence of the arising Turks made them fight with more vigor and conviction.

The Battle of Pelekanon marks a significant turning point in the history of the region. The Byzantine Empire never again tried to reclaim the lost territories on the Asian side of Bosphorus and more or less left Nicea and Nicomedia to be besieged and later incorporated into

Orhan's beylik. By 1340 Orhan had also annexed the beylik of Karasi which was the first time he had chosen to march towards Turkish neighbors. He did so because the chief had passed away and the two sons of the chief were currently warring against each other to claim the title. Many soldiers and civilians had already died when Orhan decided to intervene for the sake of peace. One of the brothers was killed and the other captured and Orhan now ruled four provinces. Most of the cities within the beylik were peaceful and many former Christians quickly embraced Islam without coercion. The region needed to be stabilized in order to build the strong state apparatus as the foundation of an empire. Orhan had put all of Bithynia and the northwestern corner of Anatolia under his control without much resistance from the population.

After his brother's death in the early 1330s, Orhan had help of his two eldest sons Suleyman and Murad in expanding the emirate. In 1341, the Byzantine Emperor Andronicus III died and left an 8-year-old successor on the throne. The following civil war created a golden opportunity for the Ottomans to march further into the declining empire and inflict some irreparable damage. The fall of the empire would take another hundred years of power struggles, but there was no way to restore it to its former glory. A six-year-long civil war broke out on the Balkans, and since peace reigned in Orhan's lands, he chose to head further west attempting to create an Ottoman road to Europe.

The Byzantine Grand Domestic John VI Kantakouzenos, who was also the young emperor's custodian and acting as regent, recognized Orhan's potential and formed an alliance with the Ottoman chief. He gave his daughter Theodora in marriage and then used Orhan's help to usurp the throne and become Emperor of Byzantine in 1347. In exchange, Orhan gained the right to plunder Thrace and he started raiding the area regularly through the peninsula of Gallipoli. His oldest son Suleyman took charge of the plundering as Orhan himself was growing older and weaker. The raiding was fruitful and the Ottomans gained both land and riches, while the Byzantine emperor let them. This attracted thousands of uprooted Turkmen to head west and join in Suleyman's expeditions. The emperor of Byzantine had not intended for the Ottomans to actually take possession of Thrace, but that was, of course, inevitable. After Suleyman made Gallipoli into a permanent base for his raiding parties across present-day Bulgaria it didn't take long until John VI was more or less forced to sign over the lands to Orhan's family, a very prestigious win. Constantinople was now surrounded by Ottoman territory, albeit still under Byzantine rule.

It was by the end of Orhan's life that his oldest son died in an accident, which took a toll on Orhan's spirit. He withdrew from power and his last years were spent living quietly in Bursa. Before he died, his youngest son whom he had with Theodora, Sehzade Halil, was kidnapped by pirates along the Aegean coast. It is unclear if they knew who they were kidnapping but when realizing, they took refuge in a Byzantine fortress in Phocaea. After finding this out, Orhan appealed to the co-emperor Andronikos IV to rescue his son and promised in return to call off debts and withdraw his support for the Kantakouzenos family. Andronikus agreed and laid siege to Phocaea, which ended in Orhan paying 30,000 ducats as a ransom for his son. Halil was released in 1359 and it was decided he would marry another Byzantine princess to strengthen the ties between the two dynasties. The imperial family hoped to see Halil as the rightful heir to the beylik since the older brother Suleyman had died.

Their expectations would soon turn into disappointment when Murad was appointed successor to the throne and not the teenager born by Theodora. Murad took over the title and started ruling the emirate after Orhan's death. Orhan was the longest living and ruling chief of all the Ottoman leaders and died in 1362 at the age of 80. Shortly after Orhan's death Murad even had his half-brother executed accused of challenging Murad for the throne. The 16-year-old had already gotten married and produced two young boys who were now left fatherless. This was perhaps the start of brotherly distrust between the heirs of the Ottoman empire. The first sultans had neglected to formulate an order of succession and it was not until a hundred years later they constituted laws. Hence the throne was up for grabs by any of the sons when a sultan died, although usually some sort of pre-agreement had been made between the generations. Out of sight from the dead father the avaricious sons almost made it a habit to challenge each other for the throne. After Murad had executed his little brother, many more were to follow his example.

Murad was now the undisputed ruler of Osman's beylik, and the first major conquest attributed to him was that of Adrianople, the third most important city of the Byzantine Empire. As more sources have been found in later year,s it is now debated when the conquest really took place, and even who actually conquered Adrianople. It has been the general consensus that Murad laid siege to the city in either 1361 or 1362, but newer research holds 1367 or 1371 as more likely. There's also a possibility that it was not Ottoman Turks who conquered the city but some other group of the roaming ghazi warriors. It is also debated regarding when Murad moved his capital from Bursa to Adrianople, the general opinion being that Murad captured the city in 1362, renamed it Erdine and made it the new capital in 1363. Other sources say that the city still belonged to Byzantium by 1366 and was conquered in the 1370s by Murad's second lieutenant Lala Sahin Pasa, who also administered the city for some time after. The same source claims that Murad himself actually didn't enter Erdine until 1377, when the Byzantine Emperor Andronikos IV needed his help in a civil war. Erdine was the military center of the Ottomans in the Balkans, but Bursa was considered the capital until the conquest of Constantinople and the rebuilding of it into a new capital.

## Murad I

Murad transformed the beylik into a sultanate in 1383 and declared himself sultan. His right hand, the second lieutenant Lala Sahin Pasa, became the governor of the western province Rumeli while Murad remained in control over Anatolia. At this point, he also instituted an army, referred to as Janissaries, and a recruiting system called Devshirme. This was possible thanks to the reorganization of the military, a seed which was planted by his uncle Alaeddin some 50 years earlier. The Janissaries were an elite infantry loyal only to the sultan. Their mission was to protect only him and in battles they were always the closest to him, forming a human shield. Originally they consisted of non-Muslim slaves, mainly Christian boys from Byzantium. Jewish boys were not taken as soldiers and Muslims could not, by law, be enslaved. Murad had instituted a tax of one fifth on all the slaves taken in war, and the idea of only taking boys fit for fighting was called Devshirme, or blood tax. The slaves went through a very strict training, first learning to speak Turkish and practicing Ottoman traditions by living with a family chosen by the sultan. The boys also were forcibly converted to Islam, forbidden from wearing a beard and lived under monastic circumstances in celibacy. They were overseen by eunuchs and trained in special schools, enhancing their personal abilities. The main difference between these and other slaves was that they were being paid for their services. This served as a motivator and kept the soldiers loyal.

The Janissaries were at first a hated institution by the subjugated Christian minorities. Rather than having their sons taken away, it happened that the parents disfigured their children so as to make them weak and unsuitable for Devshirme. But the status of the Janissaries grew. They became men of high learning and an ascetic nature, favored by the sultan. As they grew in numbers, they also became very influential in the capital and their skills as warriors made them feared far beyond the borders of the empire. The Janissary corps was the first of its kind and a groundbreaking contributor to the success of Ottoman warfare. At the time of Murad's reign, they were fewer and less respected than what they would become at a later stage, though they were quite significant for the conquering of the Balkans.

Not just the conquest of Erdine but also many other historical details in Murad's life is widely debated by historians today. Though it is difficult to prove the consecutive order of certain events in the fast-growing sultanate, it is certain that his reign was a bloody and expansive period, followed by more of the same by his successor. During the 1370s his second lieutenant and trusted friend Lala Sahin Pasa crushed the Serbian armies in the battle of Maritsa though they were heavily outnumbered. Using superior strategies and a surprise night-time attack, the Serbs were close to being annihilated and their king killed in the campaign. Little remained of the Serbian Empire and the lands were easily taken over by the Ottomans. They then aimed north and started raiding Bulgaria's southern borders. The Bulgarian king more or less acquiesced to vassalage, something that the Serbians, Macedonians and some of the Greek rulers already had done, though the Ottomans kept deprecating their borders. After capturing both Sofia and Nis by the year 1386, Murad was forced to return to Anatolia to settle rising troubles in the home province. In his wake, the bitter rulers of the Balkans formed an alliance and went to war against the Ottoman forces. Two of the Bulgarian princes, along with the Serbian Prince Lazar and more allies from Kosovo, Macedonia and Bosnia won their first battle against the Ottomans and took back Nis in 1388. Murad quickly responded by launching new campaigns in his recently conquered territories which resulted in the Battle of Kosovo in 1389.

   The Battle of Kosovo was the apogee of Murad's fighting in the Balkans and turned into a bloodbath with significant losses on both sides. It was in the midst of summer, June 1389, that the two foes met slightly north of modern-day Pristina in the open fields of Kosovo. Records of the actual battle itself are scarce, but historians have managed to reconstruct a likely chain of events thanks to written down strategies, numbers, and information from other, similar battles.

The Serbian and Turkish sources often contradict each other, and what modern history books retell about the events are based on the general assumption and what most likely is true. Murad arrived backed up by a neighboring beylik from Anatolia, and together they had mustered an army of nearly 40,000 men. The Serbian Prince Lazar had, together with allies from Kosovo and Bosnia, an army the size of 30,000 men. As some sources claim, it is also likely that the Knight Hospitaller from Croatia fought on the Serbian side, and anachronistic records state that the Serbian army was larger than Murad's. Murad had both his sons with him, Bayezid and Yakub, commanding one wing each.

Initially, it looked like the Serbs would prevail and the Ottoman forces conceded heavy losses during the first hours. However, in a frenzy of bloodthirst and revenge,

Bayezid led his wing in a counterattack towards the knights, whose heavy armor became a hindrance for their retreat. Bayezid slaughtered a great number of the Serbian soldiers, and Prince Lazar's allied Vuc Brankovic from Kosovo fled the field trying to rescue as many men as possible. At this point, Prince Lazar had probably been captured or killed in the heat of the battle. At the end, there was not much left of either army, the Serbian Prince Lazar had died, and Sultan Murad had been killed. There are three common stories about how and when he was killed - either in battle by Lazar, by one of the 12 Serbian lords who broke through Ottoman lines, or by an assassin in his own tent after the battle was won. No matter which story is true, it resulted in the oldest son Bayezid strangling his brother Yakud on the spot, so as to be the sole heir to the throne. Hence he pursued in his father's footsteps, as his father had also started his reign by killing his brother.

After the war, the Serbs didn't have enough troops left to defend their territory. Bayezid sent for more armies from the east and within a short period of time, most of the principalities became Ottoman vassals.

Murad I had died at the age of 62, and his organs were buried in the battlefield in Kosovo, while his body was transported and buried in Bursa. His legacy included a lot more than just new lands, and apart from his military reorganization, he also created the council of ministers called Divan, over which the grand vizier presided. This became the ruling political entity in the sultanate. He united the smaller emirates into two larger provinces, Rumeli and Anatolia, each ruled by a strong provincial vizier. The military court was also Murad's doing, and he introduced a legal system. At the same time, he expanded the sultanate in Anatolia but even more to the west of the Bosphorus, to include most of the Balkans and Bulgaria. When he died he left the sultanate ready to rule for his son Bayezid.

**Bayezid I**

It would seem as if much of the hard work already had been done by the time Bayezid came to power in the Ottoman Sultanate. The difficult first century of expanding and stabilizing the new state had passed, and many of the foundational institutions been formed by Murad and Orhan. The military and government had been efficiently organized and now Bayezid needed to emulate his predecessors. After the battle of Kosovo and the losses of thousands of soldiers, as well his father, Bayezid continued to raid the Balkans. He maintained the borders to the south and coerced the Albanian, Macedonian and Serbian princes into vassalage. By marrying the daughter of the deceased Prince Lazar, he established a new bond with her brother, the soon-to-be-despot Stefan Lazarevic. After endorsing Stefan he left him in charge of the Balkan territories and returned to Anatolia to settle unrest in his homelands.

In 1390 he managed to conquer six different beyliks to the north and east of his territory before the winter fell, the first time an Ottoman ruler had decided to annex Turkish lands. It was partially because of his skills as a warrior and because of his fiery temper he gained the nickname Yildirim, lightning bolt.

The annexation of the Anatolian lands didn't come without consequences. Both Turkmen loyal to the Ottoman dynasty and outside of their territories expressed dissatisfaction and Bayezid sought peace with the larger emirate Karaman in 1391. He had been using fatwas, declared by Islamic scholars, to justify the expansion into Muslim territories, but this was as far as he would come in Anatolia.

After the peace was negotiated, he turned north with some success but was in the end forced to return west where rumors of an uprising circulated. It was the Hungarian King Sigismund who had cajoled Bulgaria's Ivan Shishman, the king of one of the vassal states, and the Wallachian ruler Mircea the Old, into an anti-Ottoman coalition. News of the alliance reached Bayezid who, true to his nickname, acted swiftly and ruthlessly. The Bulgarian vassal took most of the hit from Bayezid, who recaptured the lands and beheaded Shishman while leaving the distant Hungarian King and Wallachia to be dealt with later. Bayezid had to hurry south to settle disputes and bickering between the Greek lords under his rule.

After a successful meeting in Serre in 1394, he had reinstated his power over his vassal states, and by a series of events also managed to extend his vassalage to include the city of Athens. The same year he also laid siege to the Byzantine capital Constantinople, which called for help from the Hungarian Kingdom. The siege lasted for eight years, and during most of it, Bayezid had to keep fighting on other frontiers of his sultanate.

One of the last major crusades was launched in 1396 by Pope Boniface IX. The timing was perfect for the European kingdoms to unite and form a strong threat to the Turks. The 100-year war between France and England was in a state of truce and King Richard II had just married Princess Isabella of France. Both the Brits and the Franks sent forces to join in the crusade, and so did Hungary, Bulgaria, Venice, Genoa, Croatia, Wallachia, the Holy Roman Empire and the Knights Hospitaller. It is estimated that both the Crusader forces and the Ottoman armies consisted of somewhere between 15,000–20 000 men each, but the sources all tell different stories. Some tell of armies the size of hundreds of thousands of men, and some say that the enemy force was at least twice the size of their own army. The details of the battle are questionable since historians on both sides wrote to please and aggrandize their own leaders. In fact, the actual participation of English soldiers has not been proven, and records of such an army being sent abroad at the time don't exist. Genoa and Venice were probably also more engaged in other areas under their rule, although they surely sent a smaller convoy to backup the crusaders. On the Ottoman side, numbers vary just as much, but the coalition of Serbs and Turkmen could probably be numbered to less than 20,000.

On arriving at Nicopolis on the river Danube, the crusaders laid siege to the Ottoman-controlled city. Their first mistake was not to bring any siege armaments, making any attempt to conquer the city with force futile. The crusader generals changed tactics and decided to block the exits and the port of the city with the intention of starving the citizens, and in such a way make them surrender. During the siege, there wasn't therefore much for the soldiers to do but to play games, drink wine and wait for Nicopolis to give in. When rumors of the approaching Ottoman armies reached Nicopolis the French marshal, Boucicaut threatened to cut off the ears of anyone talking about the Turkmen. He thought the rumors of approaching soldiers would deflate the morals of the troops. Hence, little did they expect that a lightning bolt was rapidly heading their way from Constantinople. When Bayezid and his Serbian ally Lazarevic were six hours away from the camp the crusaders were in the midst of a drunken dinner celebration. In stress and panic, they started executing some 1000 prisoners they had taken in the town of Rachowa, which would later add to the fury of Bayezid.

The French, Hungarian and Wallachian rulers drew a battle plan in all haste, but they couldn't agree on the details. Sending the foot soldiers in first would be an insult to the great French knights having to follow in the lead of peasants, and therefore they had to go first into battle. Sigismund argued that the Turkish vanguard was not worthy of the French knights and that his infantry should take the lead. In the end, the French lords had their will and a couple of hours later the knights rode out to face the Turkish forces. Thanks to a hill hiding the full strength of the Ottoman army, the knights once again underestimated its foes and rode straight into annihilation.

After that initial clash, the rest of the French troops threw themselves to the ground, pleading for their lives. Bayezid knew the value of French nobility, so he took them hostage and later set them free for large ransoms. King Sigismund and the Master of the Hospitallers were the only leaders able to flee, and Sigismund later accused the French of hubris and for putting pride ahead of tactics. The rest of the noblemen were taken prisoners and many of the surviving soldiers were executed as retribution of the 1,000 murdered civilians from Rachowa. After the carnage, the hostages were marched in chains all the way to Gallipoli, where they were kept in prison for two months while waiting for the news to reach Central Europe. The fleeing Sigismund had failed to negotiate the ransom for his allies since Bayezid knew the Hungarian assets were depleted. It took over a year and a half before the last generals and noblemen returned to their homes, and many of them had already died from battle wounds or poor conditions while captured.

While all this took place, Bayezid continued his siege of Constantinople half-heartedly but gave up after striking a compromise with the Emperor Manuel II. It was agreed that Bayezid should have veto in approving and confirming all the future Byzantine emperors. Bayezid left Constantinople, never to return west of Bosphorus again. There was unrest in his annexed territories in Anatolia where the newly arrived Central Asian conqueror Timur was in the midst of establishing a new Mongolian Empire. With Bayezid occupied the Balkans, Timur had managed to form a coalition of the Ottoman vassal states against their sultan. Bayezid rushed to meet him with a strong 85,000 man army consisting of Turks, Serbs, Albanians, Tartars, ghazis and janissaries and even Christians. However, the 140,000 Mongol-Turkish cavalry troops accompanied by 32 war elephants must have put some fear in the defending Ottoman allies.

Heavily outnumbered and tired from the long march, the battle couldn't have started any worse for Bayezid's armies. Two of his allied forces switched sides during the battle, and when a defeat became inevitable the Serbian troops escaped with the Ottoman Treasury and one of Bayezid's sons. Stefan Lazarevic urged Bayezid to flee, but Bayezid kept his position and continued fighting. After the battle had been lost, Bayezid was captured by the Timurids and died in prison a couple of months later. Some historians claim he was being abused while taken hostage and driven to suicide, while others claim the opposite. One of his sons, Mustafa Celebi, was also captured with him but was held in Samarkand until Timur's death in 1405.

Bayezid's death had devastating consequences for the Ottoman Sultanate. Except for Mustafa who was in prison, Bayezid had four more sons, all hungry to rule the sultanate. The youngest, Mehmed Celebi, was confirmed as a sultan by Timur, but his brothers refused to acknowledge his authority. The result would be a civil war known as the Ottoman Interregnum, which lasted for over a decade. During the years of fighting, Mustafa stayed hidden from his brothers, plotting to make his move for when they had defeated each other.

Timur had no intentions of conquering or ruling Anatolia, and after he had won the Battle of Ankara he withdrew from the territory, satisfied with leaving the beyliks divided. The Ottoman family got to keep their lands around Bursa, and no one had made any claim to their acquisitions in the Balkans. The commotion gave a window opportunity for Thessaloniki, Kosovo, and Macedonia to break free from the vassalage, but the other states remained under Ottoman rule, awaiting the next sultan. The only significant losses of the dynasty after the war were pride and the trust of their Muslim neighbors whom they had annexed and ruled.

If Bayezid had not died in prison, the damage done to his sultanate by Timur would have been easy to repair. However, Bayezid had had many sons, and there was no set order of succession within the dynasty. The eldest son had died before the Battle of Ankara, and the next in age, Mustafa, was in prison in Samarkand. Four more sons thus had potential claims to the throne, although the youngest, Mehmed, had been recognized as the new sultan by Timur before he left. Naturally, the three others opposed this appointment of their little brother, and it didn't take long before war was raging between the four of them. The ensuing civil war lasted for 11 violent years.

The sources describing what led up to and finally caused the Interregnum reveal many different storylines about Bayezid and all his sons. He himself is said to have been tortured and compelled to commit suicide in the care of Timur, while one of his wives too was abused. It is said that Mustafa was not taken captive, but mysteriously vanished during the battle and it is also said that Isa and Musa escaped by themselves, while Suleyman and Mehmed were taken care of by Bayezid's allies. Other sources tell of both Musa and Mustafa being captured, with Musa being released after Mehmed's negotiations with Timur and Mustafa when Timur himself died. The order of the brother's ages is also not fully clear, nor is how they were allied with each other during the Interregnum. The general assessment is that three of the brothers each occupied different territories in the former United Ottoman Sultanate. The oldest, Suleyman, moved to the Balkans and established his capital in Erdine. Constantinople was still the capital of the Byzantine Empire, but the lands around it were occupied by Isa, one of the middle brothers. The youngest, Mehmed, took possession of the eastern parts and tried to strike a deal to share the Anatolian territories with Isa, who promptly refused and instead signed a treaty of friendship with the Byzantine emperor. The fourth brother Musa was probably in captivity for one year until Mehmed negotiated his release. Musa then aimed for Bursa, with the aid of Mehmed, and therefore contested the territories already ruled by Isa. It was not hard for Isa to defeat Musa in one of the earliest battles of the civil war, and Musa fled to Germiyanid in Mehmed's kingdom.

Next in line stood Mehmed, with a large army from eastern Anatolia. Mehmed and Isa met in the Battle of Ulubad in 1403. The battle ended in victory for Mehmed, who proclaimed himself King of Anatolia and again united the province under one rule. Isa fled to his allies in Constantinople and later moved even further west to form a coalition with his brother Suleyman. Suleyman took the opportunity to back Isa up and sent him back to Anatolia with a large army. To no avail, Mehmed won once again, and the subsequent fate of Isa is still disputed. Some say he went into hiding, while others say he was spotted in a Turkish bath and killed by Mehmed's agents in 1406. This is usually the year considered as the year of his death.

The belligerent state between the brothers was prodded on by the surrounding entities. Other emirs, the roaming ghazis, the Byzantine Empire, the Italian city-states, and the influential upper class of Bursa all had an interest in keeping the conflict going and weakening the political, economical and geographical stability in the territories. Mehmed gained some support because he was the youngest and hence considered less dangerous than his brothers.

Suleyman, who had been sitting comfortably on his throne in Erdine, together with his Grand Vizier Candali Ali Pashar and the support of Byzantine ruler John VII Palaiologos, started worrying about his brother's accomplishments in Anatolia and decided to take action. He marched on Bursa as well as Ankara and managed to conquer them both. While Suleyman was resting and regrouping in Bursa, Mehmed and Musa formed an alliance. By sending Musa through Wallachia to Suleyman's western borders, the eldest brother suddenly had a war on two fronts on his hands. The eldest brother was overwhelmed and decided to withdraw to fight for his territories in Rumeli. With the support of both Byzantium and also the Serb Stefan Lazarevic, he defended Rumeli and took to ruling his province from Erdine without further involvements in Anatolia.

Suleyman was not an able king though and took no interest in state affairs. After his grand vizier passed away, Rumeli fell into neglect and Suleyman's flamboyant lifestyle caused him to lose support among his allies and subordinates. When the bellicose Musa came for Erdine, Suleyman had very few supporters left and the capital was easily conquered by the younger brother. Trying to escape to Byzantine lands, Suleyman was killed in 1411.

At this point, Musa and Mehmed co-ruled the Ottoman provinces between them, as had been done during the reign of Murad I. Even so, the brothers had no natural affinity for each other. Musa considered himself the sultan of Rumeli, while Mehmed considered him his vassal. This inevitably caused complications and the peace didn't last long. Musa had laid siege to Constantinople as a retribution for the Byzantine's support of Suleyman, and with the stirring conflict between the two remaining brothers, the emperor turned to Mehmed for help. Mehmed betrayed his brother and formed an alliance with Emperor Manuel II Palaiologos.

Meanwhile, Musa had support from many of his vassal states, along with Stefan Lazarevic, and the initial battles ended in Musa's favor. It wasn't until Lazarevic switched sides and Mehmed gained support from more Turkish emirs that Musa finally could be defeated and killed in the Battle of Camurlu in 1413. This left Mehmed as the sole survivor of the fighting brothers, and he could crown himself Sultan Mehmed I of both Anatolia and Rumeli. That put an end to the Ottoman Interregnum.

## Mehmed I

After the fighting was over, Mustafa, the brother in hiding, decided to emerge and play his part in the Ottoman history. Backed up by the Byzantine emperor, whose ever-changing sympathies now had turned against Sultan Mehmed, together with the old Wallachian vassal Mircea, he demanded Mehmed cede half the sultanate to him. Mehmed denied the request and defeated Mustafa quite easily in battle. Mustafa took refuge in Thessaloniki and the Byzantine emperor exiled him by request from Mehmed.

As fate had it, Mehmed's problems didn't end with the death and exile of all his brothers. The ever-conspiring Manuel II Palaiologos cajoled Mehmed's nephew to make a move against his uncle, but the plot was uncovered and the nephew was blinded for his betrayal.

After a few other uprisings and the constant hard work of keeping all his subordinates united peacefully, Mehmed died in 1421, after eight years as a sultan. By this time, it was evident that the empire had become too big for one ruler to govern, and that the threats arising on both frontiers would continue to destabilize the whole sultanate. The empire would need another reorganization to grow further, but the following sultan, Mehmed's son Murad, also was fully occupied with battles for most of his reign. Since Murad was only 16 when he ascended the throne, his uncle thought he would be an easy target to challenge. The Byzantine emperor released Mustafa from his exile under the pretense that he was the rightful heir to the throne. With the emperor's help, Mustafa also managed to conquer

Rumeli and become sultan of the province, if only for a couple of years.

  Though Murad was young, he was a capable soldier and general, trusted by his troops and allies. After being defeated in battle, Mustafa fled back and took refuge in Gallipoli, with Murat close behind. The sultan laid siege to the city, captured Mustafa, and had him hanged, an undignified way to be executed in the Ottoman tradition but justified by the disloyalty of Mustafa. The hanging was an exceptional act during Murad II's rule since he took great pride in his dynasty's chivalric forefathers. He studied old epic tales of noble caliphs and warriors, always acting in modesty and piety with a strong sense of justice. Murad traced his heritage back to the ghazi kings and modeled his own image on it. This was done to muster support for the reestablishment of a strong, unified empire with aims to expand in the name of Islam.

**Murad II**

Murad II became known as the Ghazi Sultan and was seen as not only defending Islam against the Christians but also as a defender of other, less powerful Muslim beys. Thus he gained support from Muslims both far and near. He turned his armies towards Venice, the Karamids, Serbia and finally Hungary – all of which he fought successfully. He renounced the throne to his 12-year-old son in 1444, tired of a life of fighting and pleased with his achievements.

The renunciation was, however, seen as a golden opportunity for the Hungarian Empire, together with Venice and the Holy Roman Empire, to again venture into Ottoman lands and reclaim the Balkans. The young Sultan Mehmed II realized his age and inexperience would be a disadvantage and called back his father to lead his armies. Murad II accepted unwillingly, more or less coerced, and took to fighting the Battle of Varna in the same year. Both armies suffered great casualties, and due to the extreme losses, Murad didn't realize he had won until some days after the battle. He continued his reign for seven more years, during which he won the Second Battle of Kosovo, secured the Balkan borders, fought and defeated Timur's son Shah Rokh, and also conquered the Karamanids. His last efforts as a ruler stabilized the region and also deterred the Christian armies from coming to any potential aid for Constantinople when his son would implement one of history's most famous and consequential sieges.

**Mehmed II**

## The Byzantine Empire Before the Fall of Constantinople

If the fall of Constantinople marked the end of the Byzantine Empire, it was only the apex of a long, slow decline. One place to start tracing the story of that decline is all the way back in 1341, when Emperor Andronicus III Palaeologus died and left no instructions regarding his successor. After strife between many parties, Andronicus's chief adviser, John Cantacuzenus, who had the support of the army, was crowned. Even from that moment, John Cantacuzenus understood that his empire needed help on a large scale, so in the first weeks of 1345, he made contact with the Ottoman Sultan Orhan. The two became friendly - at least on the surface - and Orhan even fell in love with John Cantacuzenus' daughter Theodora. Those two were married in 1346.

Medieval depiction of Andronicus III Palaeologus

John Cantacuzenus depicted as an emperor and a monk.

**Western depiction of Sultan Orhan**

On Easter Sunday of 1346, Stephen Dushan was crowned by the Serbian archbishop as the emperor of the Serbs and Greeks. He entered Constantinople with 1,000 men and emerged six days later, victorious in forging an agreement with John Cantacuzenus that the two men would be co-emperors. It is possible that John Cantacuzenus could have prevented the decline of the empire had he acted decisively when he first came to power, but by 1347, the problems of division and bankruptcy had compounded and Stephen Dushan was in the mix. Stephen Dushan posed a large problem because his empire was larger than the Byzantine Empire and he coveted Constantinople because his own country, Serbia, was landlocked.

Political problems had to be set aside, however, when the Black Death hit the region in 1347 and killed nearly 90% of the population. By the end of the plague's terrors, the empire was limited to Thrace and a few Aegean Islands. John Cantacuzenus attempted to consolidate his power by putting his sons in charge of certain parts of the territory, but more troubles came. Andronicus III Palaeologus' son, John V Palaeologus, had formed an alliance with the Venetians and was so successful in fighting the Byzantines that in 1347 he was crowned co-emperor. John Cantacuzenus tried unsuccessfully to depose John V Palaeologus and crown his son Matthew as co-emperor, but he did not succeed.

**Medieval depiction of John V Palaeologus**

By 1350, the Ottomans were involved directly in European affairs, including fighting with Genoa and Venice over control of trade on the Black Sea. The Ottomans took the side of Genoa, which in return offered them boats to ferry their people across the Bosporus. An unwitting John Cantacuzenus assisted Orhan's expansion efforts, and before long the Ottomans under Orhan had settled in Thrace and acquired their first stronghold in the Balkans. By the time Orhan died in 1362 and left control of the

Ottomans to his son Murad, the Ottomans controlled much of southern Thrace, the frontier line was significantly further west than it had begun, and the eastern side of the empire extended as far as Ankara because they had captured the domains of a rival Turk dynasty.

Meanwhile, John Cantacuzenus continued to lose popularity among his Byzantine citizens until he was finally was forced to retire to a monastery, but the emperor's unpopularity was not a reflection of his commitment to the empire. As John Julius Norwich writes, "few emperors worked harder for the imperial good; few possessed less personal ambition." He explains that for John Cantacuzenus, "the greatest burden was the moral and financial bankruptcy of the empire itself. The treasury was empty; the Byzantines themselves had lost heart."

When Stephen Dushan died in 1355, his Serbian empire dissolved, but the Ottomans were spreading. John V Palaeologus, who now ruled the Byzantine Empire uncontested, became so desperate for allies that he traveled to Hungary to seek help from King Louis the Great. It was unprecedented for an emperor to leave the empire except as the head of the army, but Louis, hated schismatics (members of Christian orders other than his own - in this case, hating the Byzantines' Orthodoxy in comparison to his Catholicism). John V Palaeologus was captured by the Bulgars, and though he was saved by his cousin Amadeus VI, count of Savoy, the Byzantine emperor was only aided in being returned to the throne if he agreed to submit to Amadeus' agenda: a church union. John V Palaeologus consented on a personal submission to Rome, but stated that, as far as the Byzantine people were concerned, a "union could not be imposed from above; the Emperor had no authority over the souls of his subjects." He suggested that their differences could be settled by having an ecumenical council, in which all the Christian nations would be welcome and unified, but Rome was not willing. John V Palaeologus nevertheless kept his promise of submission, and in return, he was invited to Venice, only to be detained as a debtor and essentially made a prisoner.

On September 26, 1371, the Turks destroyed the Serbian army, and with the Turks in control of Serbia and Bulgaria, Byzantium was effectively cut off from the west. John V Palaeologus hoped to keep the potential damage in check by joining forces with Sultan Murad, to the extent that John and his heir apparent, Manuel, offered increased tributes, additional military assistance, and the city of Philadelphia (the last Byzantine outpost in Asia Minor) in exchange for reinstatement as Byzantine emperor. Nonetheless, by 1381, the Byzantine Empire could no longer faithfully be called an empire but rather, in the words of John Julius Norwich, "four small states ruled by four so-called emperors and a despot". Shortly thereafter, these emperors became vassals of the Turks.

In June 1389, Sultan Murad invaded Serbia and completely defeated the Serbians, but one of the captured Boyars managed to plunge a dagger twice into the Sultan's heart and kill him near the town of Pristina. Soon after, the Serbian sovereign Lazar was brought to an Ottoman tent and decapitated. The Ottomans were victorious, but both sovereigns were dead. When the news of the murder first spread to Europe, it was received as great news for Christendom, but when the news of Serbia's defeat spread, they realized the Ottoman armies were unconquerable by anything less than a concerted Crusade. At that point, such a crusade was impossible with the resources they had.

Murad was succeeded by his son Bayezid, and the Ottoman Empire that Bayezid inherited included an occupied Serbia. The succession of Bayezid is an opportunity to remember that the Ottomans were one of many Turkish groups in Asia Minor, and that their expansion was not unopposed by other Muslims. Bayezid's succession emboldened an anti-Ottoman alliance led by his very own brother-in-law, Alaeddin Bey of Karaman. When the Ottomans pushed southward, hoping to control trade routes to the Mediterranean, Alaeddin Bey himself initiated hostilities, attempting to prevent the Ottomans' expansionist goals.

Together with the Ottomans' neighboring vassals, Stephen Lazarevic of Serbia and Manuel II Palaeologus of Byzantium, Bayezid conquered some of the last few territories in Anatolia that had held out from Ottoman control. Though he obliged to his duties to Bayezid, Manuel II wrote the following letter on his campaign, conveying his feelings about the Ottoman leader and his expansion: "Certainly the Romans had a name for the small plain where we are now when they lived and ruled here...There are many cities here, but they lack what constitutes the true splendor of a city...that is, human beings. Most now lie in ruins...not even the names have survived...I cannot tell you exactly where we are...It is hard to bear all this...the scarcity of supplies, the severity of winter and the sickness which has struck down many of our men...[have] greatly depressed me...it is unbearable...to be unable to see anything, hear anything, do anything during all this time which could somehow...lift our spirit. This terribly oppressive time makes no concession to us who regard it of prime importance to remain aloof from and to have absolutely nothing to do with what we are now involved in or anything connected with it, for we are not educated for this sort of thing, nor accustomed to enjoy it, nor is it in our nature. The blame lies with the present state of affairs, not to mention the individual [Bayezid] whose fault they are."

The Byzantines were also ordered by Bayezid to be obedient during the Ottoman siege of Philadelphia, essentially forcing the Byzantines to be instrumental in their own decline. No doubt suffering from humiliation, John V Palaeologus died on February 16, 1391, but while he was now fully in charge of the Byzantine Empire, Manuel II was nothing more than a vassal. That year, he was summoned to help another Ottoman campaign to seize the Black Sea and thus control important trade and military routes and territories.

**Medieval depiction of Manuel II**

**Sultan Bayezid I**

In 1393, Sultan Bayezid called his principal Christian vassals to his camp at Serres and Manuel obliged. Though some feared he would slay them all, he simply reprimanded them for poor governance of their territories and sent them on their way. However, the next time Bayezid summoned his vassals, Manuel refused. Bayezid interpreted his defiance as war, and indeed, Manuel had only taken the risk because he believed in the impregnability of Constantinople. He also knew that Bayezid had no navy, but to help his cause, Manuel reached out to other Christian empires for assistance. Sigismund of Hungary made a general appeal to the princes of Christendom, and this time, sensing how dire the circumstances of the Byzantine Empire were, they responded. Even the rival popes, Boniface IX in Rome and Benedict XIII in Avignon, responded.

Manuel did have good reasons to believe in Constantinople's ability to defend itself. At the end of the 14th century, Constantinople was the most impregnable city in the world, surrounded entirely by a complex and gigantic system of walls. The city's location on a triangular spit of land, guarded by the Bosporus Straits on one side and the Sea of Marmara on another, meant only one side could be approached by land. On the water-facing sides, the city had high sea walls and promontories from which the Byzantines could bombard any ships approaching the city. On the only land side, the city boasted the famous Theodosian Walls, which were constructed in the 5th century and were fortified by alternating moats with stone walls. The innermost wall stood 90 feet high and was more than 30 feet thick. These walls had protected Constantinople from siege by the Avars, Arabs, Rus' and Bulgars.

Even if insurgents were able to get beyond the walls, the Byzantines had a secret weapon called Byzantine Fire or Greek Fire, a burning substance launched from catapults that splashed when landed and stuck to flesh. It could not be doused with water, so it was especially useful to the Byzantines in naval battles because it could keep burning on water. The makeup of this mysterious substance remains a matter of debate, but suggestions include naptha, quicklime, sulfur, niter, and pine resin. Historian Tamim Ansary has labeled it "some primitive form of napalm."

**A restored section of Constantinople's walls.**

That spring, Bayezid embarked on his first attempt at a

siege of Constantinople, and his first step in conducting a siege was to build a fortress a little more than 3 miles up the Bosporus from Constantinople. The castle was on the Asian side of the river at its narrowest point and was named Güzelcehisar ("Beauteous Castle"), and today it is called Anadolu Hisarı. The castle was finished by 1397.

While constructing a castle that would be integral to his siege of Constantinople, Bayezid tried to threaten Hungary, his most dangerous enemy in the Balkans, by seizing Macedonia in 1395 and then the city of Nikopol, giving the Ottomans control of the Balkans south of the Danube. From Nikopol, he sent his men into Hungary for the first time, and they raided far and wide. Alaeddin Bey, the Sultan's brother-in-law, made it known that he was not impressed by Bayezid's forceful expansion, but he paid for this pride with his life, and afterwards Bayezid claimed the Karamanid emirate for himself.

Constantinople's walls had kept many foreign invaders out, and it continued to hold out against Bayezid as Manuel sought help from Europe. In 1399, Charles VI of France sent 12,000 gold francs and a force of 1,200 men, led by the greatest French soldier of the day, Jean le Maingre, Marshal Boucicault. Boucicault managed to get through the Ottoman blockade and reach Constantinople in September, but he quickly realized that any effective army would have to be organized on a far larger scale than what was available between his men and Manuel's. Jean le Maingre insisted that the emperor himself go to Paris and plead his cause before the French king. Manuel agreed and was fêted all along the way by Christian leaders who newly supported him and viewed him as the defender of Christendom. When he arrived in Paris, an entire wing of the Louvre had been redecorated for him, but King Charles still refused to consider a full-scale international Crusade on behalf of the beleaguered

Byzantines.

**Contemporary painting of Charles VI of France**

Manuel stayed in Europe, traveling to appeal to England's King Henry IV, the kings of Aragon and Portugal, the Pope and Antipope. Though they received him warmly, he failed to generate the scale of support he desired, and the money collected for Manuel around England allegedly disappeared. This left Manuel in low spirits until Seigneur Jean de Chateaumorand, who Bouricault had left in charge of Constantinople, arrived with the news that the Mongols under Tamerlane had destroyed the Ottoman army and Bayezid had been taken prisoner. Tamerlane, known as the most ruthless and bloodthirsty of the Mongols, saw himself and his army as the descendents of Genghis Khan, while the Ottomans saw themselves as the heirs of the Sejluk state. After Bayezid's death at the hands of Tamerlane, he became revered as a tragic figure, as Ottoman historians passed down a legend of Tamerlane forcing him to sit in an iron cage as they crossed Anatolia, but the more likely story is that Bayezid committed suicide shortly after being taken prisoner.

Bayezid's death initiated a decade of friction between his sons, all vying for the prize of being Sultan, because Turks had no law of primogeniture (right of succession to the firstborn son). Prince Süleyman, the oldest of Bayezid's sons, took quick actions to prevent his Balkan vassals (Byzantine, Serbian, and Latin) from taking advantage of the disintegration of the Ottoman regime, and he also quickly started negotiations in order to prevent them from exercising historical claims to territories within his weakened realm. In 1403, however, after he had been unable to regain power, Süleyman was forced to make previously unthinkable territorial concessions. In the Treaty of 1403, Süleyman released Byzantine vassalage, returned Thessalonica to Byzantine control, released Byzantine prisoners, and agreed that Turkish vessels would no longer enter Constantinople's harbor without permission. In essence, Manuel had found himself in a much better position while overseas.

After Bayezid's death, his son Mehmed retired to his base in north-central Anatolia, only to re-emerge when Tamerlane returned eastward in 1403, but for the next few years, Süleyman ruled with stability after his treaty with the Byzantine Empire. He expanded his reign to include Bursa and Ankara in 1404, and achieved high enough status that some historians consider him to have been a sultan, Süleyman I.

However, in 1411, Süleyman's younger brother Musa captured Adrianople, after which Süleyman was taken prisoner and instantly strangled. The field of contestants for succession to the Ottoman throne was now reduced to Mehmed and Musa, but for now, Musa was the more powerful brother. Almost as quickly as he put his brother to death, Musa abrogated the Treaty of 1403 and declared his brother's various concessions null and void.

Manuel had been pleased with the instability that the brothers' competition brought on and did his best to prolong it, but in 1411, Musa tried to lay siege to Constantinople because Süleyman's son Orhan had taken refuge there, and Musa was worried that he would pose a threat. Desperate for help in staving off Musa, the Byzantine emperor dispatched an embassy to Mehmed's court at Brusa. An alliance with Manuel seemed a small price to pay for Mehmed, so he led a huge army against Musa and defeated him at Camurlu in Serbia on July 5, 1413. Musa was strangled in the battle, and with that, the succession went to Mehmed, now called Sultan Mehmed I.

**A medieval depiction of Mehmed I**

Mehmed was so grateful to be the unopposed leader of the Ottomans that he wrote the following letter to Manuel: "Go and say to my father the emperor of the Romans that from this day forth I am and shall be his subject, as a son to his father. Let him but command me to do his bidding, and I shall with the greatest pleasure execute his wishes as his servant." As long as they were both alive, there was no change in the friendly status quo between Mehmed and Manuel.

Mehmed's first goal was winning the allegiance of the

Anatolian communities who had gained independence since Tamerlane's victory. He met with resistance from Karaman and Cüneyd (emir of Aydın), but he eventually captured Cüneyd's territory and appointed Cüneyd the governor of Nikopol, in keeping with the tradition of Ottoman governance to appoint former rebels to administrative posts in hopes of keeping them content and docile. Because of Mehmed's successes, Manuel's position was further weakened, even as the two remained outwardly friendly.

The Ottomans met opposition of a new kind in 1416 with the rise of several cult-like charismatic figures, most notably Sheikh Bedreddin, a member of a religious hierarchy who was born of mixed Christian-Muslim heritage and preached "oneness of being", the idea that there was no difference between religions and prophets. He was so captivating that he successfully brought about a revolt in Rumeli, but the revolt was short lived, and Mehmed's men apprehended and executed him. The story of Sheikh Bedreddin later inspired Turkish poet Nazim Hıkmet in his anti-fascist struggle in the 1930's, and Bedreddin was the topic of Hıkmet's epic poem *The Epic of Sheikh Bedreddin*.

When Mehmed died suddenly in a horse accident in 1421, his successor was his son, Sultan Murad II. As he came to power, Murad had to fight off two "false Mustafas" who claimed the right to the throne on the grounds that they were Mehmed's lost brother Mustafa. The first of the two was beaten in battle, and the second was strangled on the grounds that no sacrifice was too great for the maintenance of the public order.

**Murad II**

Sultan Murad II continued his father's efforts to rebuild the Ottoman state, and though pesky Karaman remained independent, Murad consolidated his rule.

This also meant the period of respite for the Byzantines came to an end. A holy man foretold to Murad II that Constantinople would fall on August 24, so Murad waited all summer until that date to make an attack on the city. Fortunately for the Byzantines, the city's defenses again held, and rightly sensing that Murad II was not a leader who was willing to work with him, the Byzantine emperor - now very old - conspired to put the Sultan's youngest son, Mustafa, on the Ottoman throne. Shortly thereafter, however, Manuel was bedridden by a stroke. He resigned from the throne, became a monk, and died in July of 1425.

Upon Manuel's death, John VIII Palaeologus became the sole leader of the Byzantines, but by this time, Constantinople was a dismal place. It had no more than 50,000 inhabitants, was economically desperate, suffering from famine, and had a devalued economy. Every day saw a further decrease in manpower for the defense of the city's land walls, and the situation was so ugly that four of Manuel's sons had chosen to flee the city altogether and head for the Despotate of the Morea (a province of the empire that included most of southern Greece's Peloponnesian peninsula) because they believed the despotate was even more protected and defensible than the walled city.

**A medieval painting of John VIII Palaeologus**

From 1424-1426, Murad attacked his vassal states of Wallachia and Serbia to prevent them from joining forces with Hungary and Venice, and the Ottomans proceeded to engage in a land-grabbing game of chicken against Hungary. It ended with a treaty in 1428, but by then the frontier lines of the two empires were closer than they had ever been. After that, a war between Venice and the Ottomans was declared in 1429. The city fell to Murad in 1430, but with its capture Murad allowed a treaty that prevented looting, restored its inhabitants, began reconstruction efforts, and converted only two of the city's churches to mosques - a sign of the city's still small Muslim population.

With those conquests behind him, the power struggle in the Balkans became the Sultan's priority. Before the Ottomans' treaty with Hungary had even expired, the empire began movement into Albania. However, the empire's focus in the Balkans meant that the emir of Karaman, Ibrahim Bey, saw an opportunity to attack certain territories in Anatolia, but his movements merely led to more territorial gains for the Ottomans, even though they still lacked the resources to fully subjugate Karaman. The Balkans occupied Murad for the remainder of his reign; his next success was that the key stronghold of Belgrade succumbed in 1440 after a six-month siege.

While he was active in the Balkans, Murad also stayed busy fighting the Byzantines. Recommencing his efforts to finally subdue Constantinople, Murad captured Thessalonica, the second largest city in the Byzantine Empire, in a matter of hours. Now sensing dire straits, Pope Martin V summoned a council of the church to meet at Basel in 1431, and to John VIII Palaeologus, this seemed like a ray of hope because the Byzantines suddenly had the opportunity to appeal to Christian nations for help. The council got off to a bad start, distracted by competition between the emperor and the pope, but by the end of the meeting, the church was theoretically reunited in 1439, undoing its 375-year-old schism (at least on paper). Even still, the Orthodox establishment was divided about whether to support the union, and Central Europe remained at odds with the Latins of the Mediterranean, but this meant that the pope would raise his promised crusade against Byzantium's enemies.

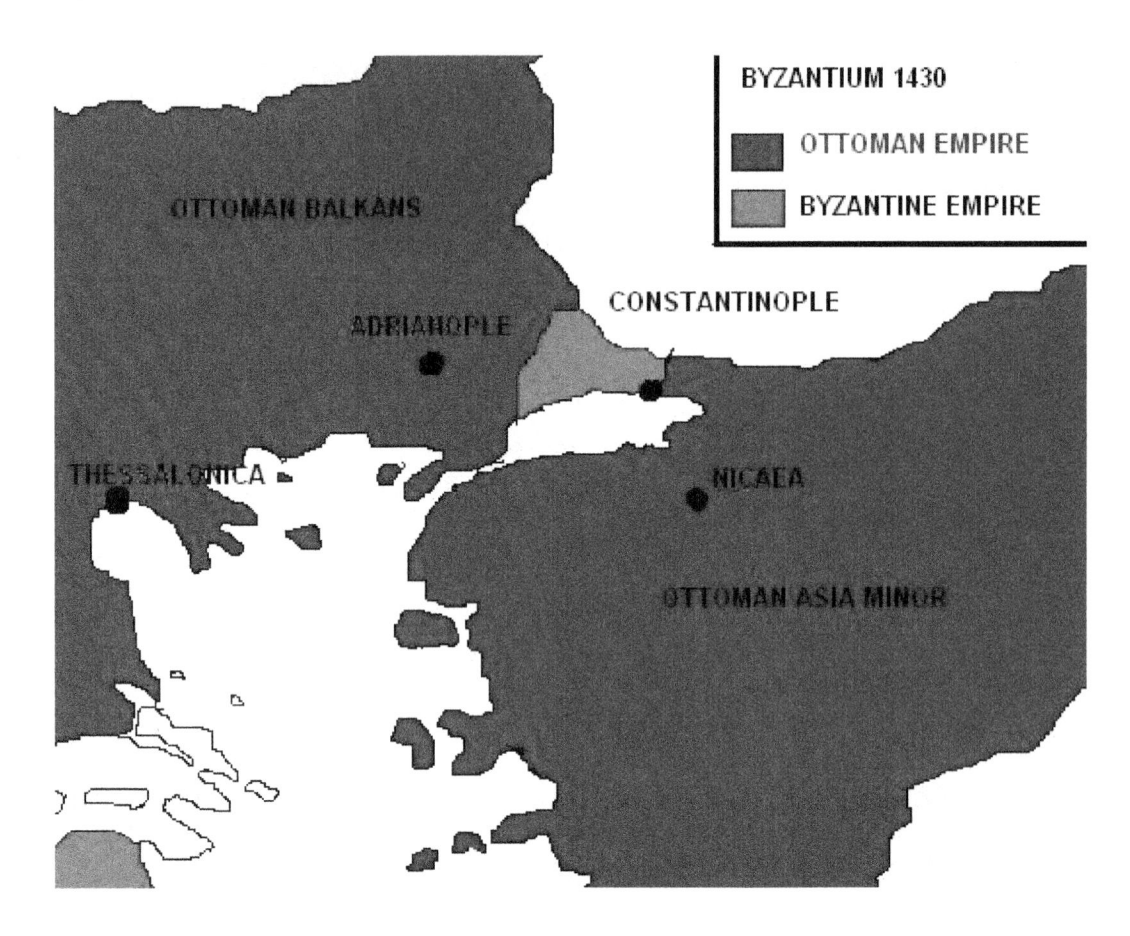

**The extent of the Byzantine and Ottoman Empires in 1430**

Hungarians formed the bulk of the crusade, and an additional fleet was provided by the Venetians, the Duke of Burgundy, and the Pope. These forces set off in the summer of 1443. That December, Sofia surrendered, and several smaller subsequent victories were enough to alarm the Sultan. The Sultan subsequently offered a truce, and when the Pope heard about the truce, he communicated to the Hungarian King Ladislas that he was no longer obligated to assist the Byzantines. At the time, Ladislas was ready to go and was expecting the fleet to come to Hungary so that they could push forward, but the fleet was busy fighting the Ottomans, preventing Ladislas from crossing the Bosporus.

Around the same time Central Europe signed the 10-year truce with Murad in 1444, the sultan summoned his son Mehmed to Edirne, the Ottoman capital, and announced plans to give up the throne. His motive remains unknown and is still a matter of speculation among historians. Perhaps he was tired out from 20 years of rule, or perhaps he was saddened by the recent death of his older brother, but whatever the case, his abdication and passing of the throne to his 12 year old son was taken by his competitors as a sign of weakness to be exploited. Ironically, Mehmed II was the son of a slave girl from a Turkish harem and was thus probably Christian, given that most women in Turkish harems were Christian girls from the Caucasus.

Absolved by the Pope of their duties to the oath, the Hungarian and Polish leaders swore fake oaths at the signing of the truce, but shortly after, crusading Hungarians crossed the Danube and marched to the

Black Sea coast. Only George Brankovic of Serbia declined to join, because Murad had promised Serbia independence. As they advanced, there was a great sense of fear in Edirne. Because Mehmed was so young, Murad had put his trusted vezir, Çandarlı Halil Pasha, in charge of overseeing him. The Çandarlı family had been with the Ottomans as first ministers since the reign of Murad I, but there were other "professional Ottomans" who were jealous of Çandarlı Halil Pasha's pre-eminent position and wanted something more than the stable state governing Anatolia and Rumeli toward which Murad had been directing the empire.

Çandarlı Halil Pasha was reluctant to allow the enthusiastic young Sultan to lead an army against the crusaders, and alarmed at the civil unrest in Edirne, he felt he had only one choice: to call back Murad. Murad didn't enter the city but led his army directly against the Hungarians. During the fighting, King Ladislas was killed, and the Hungarian troops fled. By November 1444, the crusaders had been completely crushed, putting an end to the crusade.

This was a great humiliation for John VIII

Palaeologus, who died two weeks later. Since he died childless, envoys decided that his successor would be his brother Constantine. However, Constantine XI Dragases could never be formally crowned because since the council of Florence in 1439, the Orthodox Church had been in schism, conflicted between the pro-union and anti-union sides.

# Medieval depiction of Constantine XI Dragases

After beating back the crusaders, Murad left power again, only to be called out of retirement a second time to deal with an insurrection caused by Mehmed debasing the Ottoman currency by more than 10%, which had put pressure on salaried state employees whose paychecks were suddenly worth less than before. However, upon Murad's return, many believed the Ottoman state had two sultans, with Mehmed ruling Rumeli and Murad ruling Anatolia. Ultimately, the protestors, demanding that Mehmed be removed from power, got their way; Mehmed would be out of power until Murad's death in 1451.

## The Fall of Constantinople

From the moment Mehmed finally succeeded to the Ottoman throne for good in 1451, he took no chance to be vulnerable. For instance, when Murad's widow arrived to congratulate him on his succession, Mehmed received her warmly, but when she returned to her harem she found that her infant son had been drowned in the bath.

That same year, Mehmed moved to secure his borders.

He renewed his treaty with Brankovic, leader of Serbia, and created a three-year treaty with Hunyadi, regent of Hungary. He also confirmed a treaty with Venice that his father had made in 1446. All of this would also help further his designs on Constantinople, which the Ottomans had ample reason for coveting. Control of the Bosporus would be extremely advantageous, and control of the Byzantine territory would bring large financial benefits in the form of taxation to the Ottomans. The Ottomans even described the city as their "red apple", an expression for their ultimate aspiration.

Mehmed's attack would be the 13th attempt at conquest against Constantinople, and he intended to do it right. In 1451, he began to build a fortress on the Bosporus at the place where the channel was at its narrowest, opposite Sultan Bayezid's Anadolu Hisar castle. Between the two castles, the Ottomans now had complete control of the Bosporus, which provided them with an ideal base from which to attack Constantinople from the northeast. Emperor Constantine sent embassies to speak with the Ottomans, but they were executed on the spot. Every passing ship was inspected, and when one Venetian ship disobeyed, everyone was killed.

In 1453, Mehmed told his advisors that his empire was not safe as long as Constantinople remained in Christian hands. He began to gather an army in Thrace, and every Ottoman regiment, along with hordes of mercenaries, were recruited; all in all, there were 80,000 regular troops and 20,000 *bashi-bazouks* ("others"), though some historians estimate there were as many as 160,000 troops. Furthermore, the year before, a German engineer called Urban had offered to build the Ottomans a cannon that would blast any walls, so the Ottomans paid for and received the weapon three months later. They then demanded one twice the size and received it in January 1453. It was 27 feet long and 8 inches thick, with a muzzle that was 2.5 feet across, making it capable of shooting a ball some 1,300 pounds a distance of over a mile. 200 men helped the cannon make its journey south to the outside of Constantinople's walls, and their manpower was also needed for smoothing out the road and reinforcing bridges.

**Fausto Zorano's painting, *Mehmet II conquering Constantinople***

Orthodox Easter 1453 was on the 1st of April, and on April 5th, Mehmed pitched a tent and sent a message to Constantine - one required under Islamic law - offering to spare all subjects in return for immediate surrender. He received no reply, so the cannon opened fire the next day. The people of Constantinople were not surprised, as they had worked in previous months on their city's defenses, but they were sorely lacking in resources. At their disposal, they had only eight Venetian vessels, five Genoese, and one vessel each from Ancona, Catalonia, and Provence. From the Byzantine Empire's own navy, there were only 10 vessels, meaning they only had 26 ships total. In terms of manpower, there were only 4,983 able-bodied Greeks and 2,000 foreigners, much too few to stand guard along 14 miles of wall, let alone face the 100,000 strong Ottoman army.

Nonetheless, all the defenders were in their places when the firing started. The emperor and Giovanni Giustiniani, the Genoese captain, were in command of the most vulnerable section, the area of the wall that crossed the valley of the little river Lycus about a mile from the northern end. The sea walls were less thoroughly manned than the land walls, but their garrisons also served as lookouts, reporting on the movements of the Turkish ships.

Despite these defenses, the Sultan was subjecting the land walls to a bombardment unprecedented in the history of siege warfare. By the evening of that first day, Mehmed II and the Ottoman troops had pulverized a section near the Charisius Gate, after which his soldiers tried to smash their way through, but it held. They went back to their camp at nightfall, and the Byzantines rebuilt it overnight.

Mehmed decided to hold his fire until he could bring

reinforcements, and the bombardment resumed on April 11, continuing 48 more days uninterrupted. The larger cannon could only be fired once every two or three hours, but the damage was enormous, and within a week, the outer wall across the Lycus had collapsed in several places. The Byzantines worked ceaselessly to repair it, but the damage continued.

On April 20, ships from Genoa arrived off the Hellespont. Because Sultan Mehmed was determined to amass the strongest possible naval force outside Constantinople, he had left those straits unguarded, so the arriving ships were able to enter into the Marmara unhindered. As they arrived, the Sultan rode around the head of the Golden Horn to give the order personally to his admiral, Süleyman Baltoglu, that they were absolutely not to be allowed to reach the city. Baltoglu prepared to attack, but there was a strong southerly breeze, and his ships were unmanageable against the heavy swell. His overwhelmed captains were virtually defenseless against the deluge of arrows and javelins that greeted any approach, so they were forced to stand by as the ships sailed serenely toward the Golden Horn. When the wind dropped, Baltoglu gave the order to ram the Genoese ships and board them, but Turkish ships rode low in the water, so even when they successfully rammed the other vehicle, climbing into it was impossible. The Genoese sailors were also equipped with large axes and used them to take off the hands and heads of any who wished to enter. Ultimately, the Genoese captains lashed their ships together and were able to move toward the Horn as a giant floating fortress; a few hours later, in the middle of the night, they entered the city.

Sultan Mehmed II had watched every moment of the battle from land and was so furious with its outcome that he ordered Baltoglu's execution. The admiral avoided death after his subordinates testified to his courage, but he was nevertheless sent packing. The Sultan next set his sights on the Golden Horn. He had already put his engineers to work on a road running behind Galata, from the Marmara shore, over the hill near what is now Taksim Square, and down into the Horn itself. The engineers and laborers had cast iron wheels and metal tracks, and the carpenters were hard at work building wooden cradles that could hold the keels of moderate-sized vessels. It was a remarkable undertaking, and on Sunday, April 22, the Genoese colony in Galata watched with astonishment as 70

Turkish ships were hauled in by teams of oxen over the 200 foot hill and lowered into the Horn.

**Fausto Zorano's painting, *Mehmed II at the siege of Constantinople*. This one depicts Ottoman troops transporting their fleet overland to the Golden Horn.**

The Byzantines could not believe what was happening, and they no longer had a secure harbor, which also meant that they now had three and a half more miles of sea wall to defend, including the section breached by the Crusaders in 1204. Byzantine attempts to attack the Ottoman navy failed, while initial frontal assaults by the Ottomans also failed. Near the end of April, the defenders ostentatiously beheaded hundreds of Ottomans atop the walls as a sign for the invading army, but they would not be deterred. A Venetian in Constantinople at the time wrote in his diary, "They found the Turks coming right up under the walls and seeking battle, particularly the Janissaries...and when one or two of them were killed, at once more Turks came and took away the dead ones...without caring how near they came to the city walls. Our men shot at them with guns and crossbows, aiming at the Turk who was carrying away his dead countryman, and both of them would fall to the ground dead, and then there came other Turks and took them away, none fearing death, but being willing to let ten of themselves be killed rather than suffer the shame of leaving a single Turkish corpse by the walls."

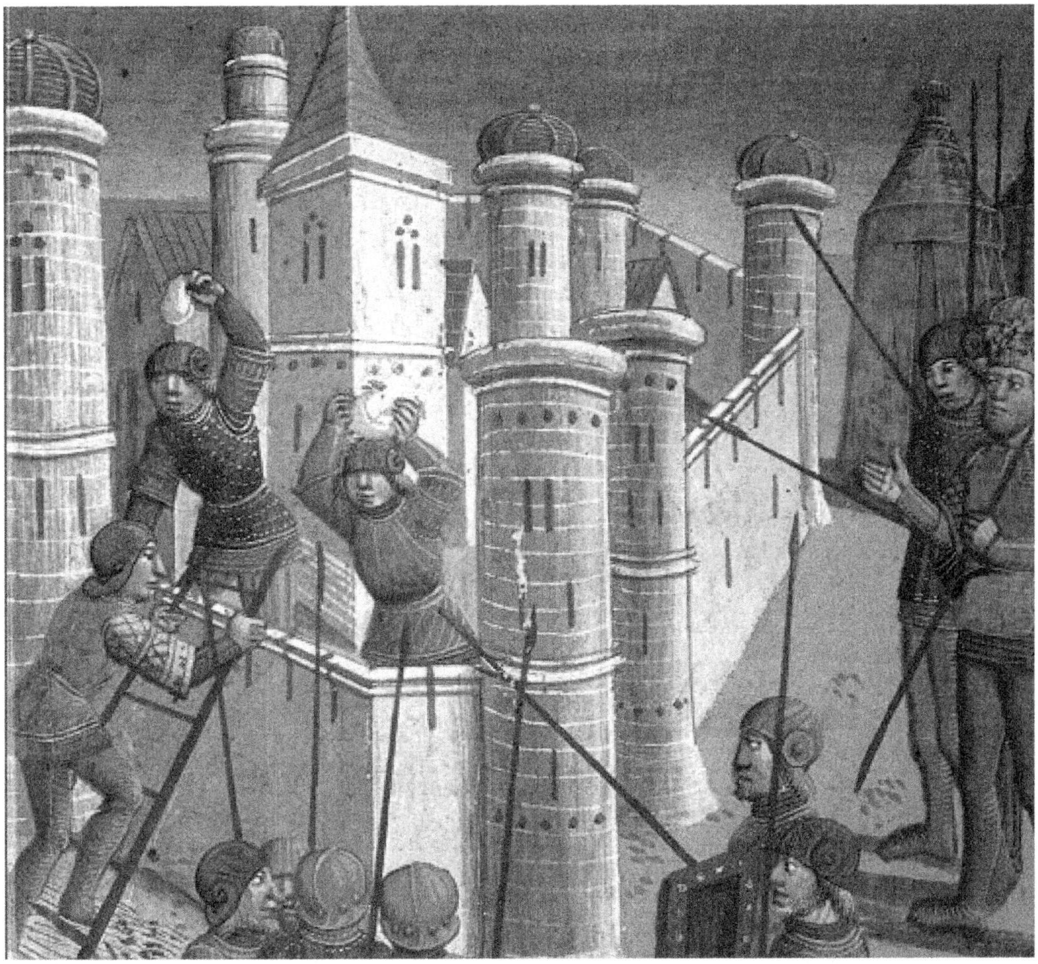

**Medieval depictions of the siege.**

 By the beginning of May, Constantine knew they would not hold out much longer; they were running out of food, and his troops were taking more and more time off of defending the city in order to find food for their families. His last faint hope was a promised Venetian relief mission, but he did not know whether it was actually on its way, what it held, or how big it was. He also did not know when it would come or how it would get through the Golden Horn, now that the Ottomans controlled it. He felt that his fate lay in the answers to these questions, so before midnight on May 3, a Venetian ship flying the Turkish flag and carrying a crew of 12 dressed in Turkish disguise slipped out.

Meanwhile, the Ottomans had given up on frontal attacks and were trying more traditional siege tactics, including tunneling under the walls to plant mines, not to mention the constant bombardment. The Byzantines dug counter-mines to locate and stop the Turkish tunnels, and they succeeded in destroying several Turkish attempts underground. Growing impatient, Mehmed sent a letter to Constantine on May 21 offering to let the people inside survive if they surrendered, and also letting Constantine head to the Peloponnese, which would be virtually the only remaining Byzantine possession. Constantine was willing to assent to the conditions, but not for the price of Constantinople, replying, "Giving you though the city depends neither on me nor on anyone else among its inhabitants; as we have all decided to die with our own free will and we shall not consider our lives."

However, two days later, when the secret Byzantine ship returned on May 23rd, its captain reported that they had combed the Aegean for weeks but had seen no trace of the promised Venetian relief expedition. Historian John Julius Norwich described the scene: "and so they had returned, knowing full well that they were unlikely to leave the city alive. Constantine thanked each one personally, his voice choked with tears."

There were also omens, or at least so they were interpreted by the Byzantines. On May 22 there was a lunar eclipse, and days later, as the holiest icon of the Virgin was being carried through the streets as an appeal to her intercession, it slipped from its platform. The morning after that, the city was shrouded in fog, which was unheard of at the end of May, and that same night the dome of St. Sophia was suffused with an unearthly red glow from the base to the summit, something that was even disturbing to Mehmed. His astrologers assured him that it was a sign that the building would soon be illuminated by the True Faith, and the Byzantines took it as a sign that the Spirit of God had deserted their city. Constantine's ministers begged him to leave the capital while there was still time and lead the empire from the Morea until he could recover the city. He fainted just as they spoke this suggestion; but when he recovered, he was determined as ever to not leave his people.

Meanwhile, the Sultan held a council of war on May 26, where he declared that the siege had continued long enough and that the time had come for a final assault. He announced that the following day would be filled with preparations, and the one after with rest and prayer, but they would begin the attack the morning of May 29, and they made no effort to conceal their plans from the Byzantines. They prepared for the next 36 hours without interruption, even lighting huge flares at night to help the soldiers with their labors. Then, at dawn on the 28th, they ceased. Mehmed set off on a day-long tour to inspect their preparations, finishing late in the evening and exhausted.

Inside the city, work on the city walls continued, but the people also gathered for one last collective appeal to God. Bells pealed, and the most sacred icons and precious relics were carried out to join a long spontaneous procession passing through the streets and along the whole length of the walls. They paused for special prayers where they expected the Ottoman artillery to concentrate particularly heavily. When the procession finished, the Emperor summoned his commanders and told his Greek subjects that there were four causes worth sacrificing one's life: his faith, his country, his family, and his sovereign. The Emperor told them they must be prepared to give their lives for all four tomorrow, and that he was prepared to sacrifice his own life. Next, he turned to the Italians and thanked them for their service. He told them that they and the Greeks were now one people, and that with God's help they would be victorious.

At dusk on the 28th, people from all over the city made their way to the Church of Holy Wisdom - St. Sophia, the spiritual center of Byzantium - for the last service of vespers ever to be held in it. Virtually every man, woman and child who was not on duty that evening gathered in the Hagia Sophia to take the Eucharist and pray for deliverance. The Emperor arrived and asked for forgiveness for his sins from every bishop present, both Catholic and Orthodox, and then took communion. Later, after all the candles were out and the church was entirely dark, he spent time in prayer before returning home for a last farewell to his household. Around midnight, he rode the length of the land walls to assure himself that everything was ready.

**Picture of the Hagia Sophia taken by Arild Vågen**

Mehmed gave his signal at 1:30 in the morning on the 29th, and suddenly the silence was shattered. The Turks made their advance known with blasts of trumpets, hammering of drums, and bloodcurdling war cries. The Byzantine church bells pealed in response. The final battle had begun.

Mehmed knew that to succeed, he could not allow the Byzantines any rest. He first sent forward his mercenary soldiers, the *bashi-bazouks*, who were poorly armed and poorly trained, but they commanded some terrifying initial force. They flung themselves against the walls for two hours. Then, shortly before four in the morning, Mehmed called for the second wave of the attack, made by several regiments of Anatolian Turks who were significantly better trained and disciplined. They nearly forced entry, but the defenders - led by the Emperor himself - closed around them, killed many, and forced them back.

Mehmed determined that victory must be won not by the Anatolians but by his very own elite regiment of Janissaries. He next sent them into battle, offering the Byzantines no time to rest. The Ottoman troops advanced swiftly across the plain, hurling themselves at the stockades and hacking away at the supports. They also put up scaling-ladders to climb the walls. Instead of attempting to use them, however, these Janissaries had the opportunity to alternate with a fourth round of troops and rest while they waited for their next turn. The defenders, short-handed and exhausted, had no opportunity. They could not last much longer, but the walls still hadn't given way.

As if the defenders didn't have enough problems, they were struck with bad luck literally when shortly after dawn, Giovanni Giustiniani, the Genoese general who had been guarding the wall's weakest point with the emperor, was struck by lightning. In excruciating pain, he was carried to a Genoese ship in the harbor, but before the gate could be relocked, Mehmed saw the opening and sent in another wave of Janissaries. They forced the Greeks to retreat to the inner wall, and once they were caught between the two rows of walls, they were trapped and highly vulnerable. Many were slaughtered in place.

A short distance to the north, both sides could see a Turkish flag now flying over a tower. An hour before the slaughter between the fortifications, a group of Turkish mercenaries had found a small door, half-hidden at the foot of a tower, that was unlocked. It was a sally-port through which the Genoese had executed several effective raids on the Turkish camp, but now the *bashi-bazouks* mercenaries managed to force it open and make their way to the top of the tower. They hoisted their flag, left the door open for others to follow, and Turkish regiments poured in through all the open breaches. Emperor Constantine plunged right into the fray and was never seen again.

**Theophilos Hatzimihail's depiction of fighting inside Constantinople. Constantine is depicted on the white horse.**

By early morning, there were scarcely any living defenders. All the surviving Greeks had raced home to try to protect their families from the Ottomans' raping and pillaging, the Venetians were racing to the harbor, and the Genoese were trusting in the relative security of Galata. The Genoese found the Horn by and large quiet, while the Venetians had no trouble getting out of the harbor, into the Marmara, and out to the open sea.

As was often the custom in the Middle Ages, the Ottomans were ruthless in their ransacking. By noon, the streets were full of running blood, women and children were raped or stabbed, and churches, icons, and books were destroyed. The Empire's holiest icon, the virgin Hodegetria, was hacked into four pieces and destroyed. One writer said that blood flowed in the city "like rainwater in the gutters after a sudden storm", and that the bodies of both Turks and Byzantines floated in the sea "like melons along a canal".

The worst massacre was at the Hagia Sophia, where services were underway when the Turks began attempting to raze the church. The Christians shut the great bronze doors, but the Turks smashed their way in. The congregation was all either massacred on the spot or carted away to a Turkish prison camp. The priests tried to continue with mass until they were killed at the altar. Some Christians believe that a few of them managed to grab the patens and chalices and disappear in to the southern wall of the sanctuary, to wait until the city became a Christian city again, at which time they would resume the service right where it was left off.

Sultan Mehmed had promised his soldiers the

traditional three days of looting, but by evening there was nothing left, and he called it off to little protest.

The historian and administrator Tursun Bey provided the sole detailed contemporary account of the siege in the Ottoman language:

> "Once the cloud of smoke of Greek fire and the soul of the Fire-worshipping Prince had descended over the castle 'as though a shadow,' the import was manifest: the devout Sultan of good fortune had, as it were, 'suspended the mountain' over this people of polytheism and destruction like the Lord God himself. Thus, both from within and without, [the shot of] the cannons and muskets and falconets and small arrows and arrows and crossbows spewed and flung out a profusion of drops of Pharaonic-seeming perspiration as in the rains of April - like a messenger of the prayers of the righteous - and a veritable precipitation and downpouring of calamities from the heavens as decreed by God. And, from the furthest reaches below to the topmost parts, and from the upper heights down

to ground level, hand-to-hand combat and charging was being joined with a clashing and plunging of arms and hooked pikes and halberds in the breaches amidst the ruin wrought by the cannon.

On the outside the Champions of Islam and on the inside the wayward ones,

pike to pike in true combat, hand-to-hand;

Now advancing now feinting, guns [firing] and arms drawn,

Countless heads were severed from their trunks;

Expelling the smoke of the Greek fire, a veritable cloud

of sparks was rained on the Champions of Islam by the infidels;

Ramming into the castle walls, the trenches in this manner,

They set off the Greek fire, the enemies;

[In turn] they presented to the bastion their

hooked pikes,

   Drawn, they were knocking to the ground the engaged warriors,

   As if struck in the deepest bedrock by the digging of a tunnel

   It seemed that in places the castle had been pierced from below.

   By the early part of the forenoon, the frenzy of the fiery tumult and the dust of strife had died away."

**Fausto Zorano's painting, *Mehmed II, Entering to Constantinople***

George Sphrantzes, who was in Constantinople when it fell, wrote about the aftermath: "On the third day after the fall of our city, the Sultan celebrated his victory with a great, joyful triumph. He issued a proclamation: the citizens of all ages who had managed to escape detection were to leave their hiding places throughout the city and come out into the open, as they were remain free and no question would be asked. He further declared the restoration of houses and property to those who had abandoned our city before the siege, if they returned home, they would be treated according to their rank and religion, as if nothing had changed."

  Perhaps most notably, after the siege was complete, Mehmed, Tursun Bey, the empire's chief ministers, imams, and the Janissaries rode to the Hagia Sophia. Mehmed picked up a handful of earth and sprinkled it over his turban as he entered as a gesture of humility, and as he approached the altar, he stopped one of the soldiers he saw hacking at the building's marble and informed him that looting did not apply to public buildings. He then commanded the senior imam to ascend to the altar and proclaim the name of Allah. With nothing more than the removal of Christian paraphernalia and their replacement with Muslim pulpits and minarets, the legendary Hagia Sophia became a mosque. The simplicity of the transformation was at once delicate and brutal, as evidenced by the way it's referred to among the Western world and the

Turks. In the Christian world, the events are known as "the Fall", but for the Ottomans of history and the Turks of today, it was and remains "the Conquest."

**Online Resources**

Other books about Rome by Charles River Editors

Other books about ancient history by Charles River Editors

Other books about Middle East history by Charles River Editors

**Further Reading about the Fall of Rome**

Alföldy, Géza. Urban life, inscriptions, and mentality in late antique Rome. In Urban Centers and Rural Contexts in Late Antiquity, Thomas S. Burns and John W. Eadie (eds.). Michigan State University Press 2001. ISBN 0-87013-585-6.

Ammianus. The History. Trans. J. C. Rolfe. Loeb Classical Library, Vol. I, 1935.

Bowersock, Glen, Peter Brown, Oleg Grabar. Interpreting Late Antiquity: essays on the postclassical world. Belknap Press of Harvard University Press, 2001. ISBN 0-674-00598-8.

Brown, Peter. The Making of Late Antiquity, Harvard University Press, 1978.

Burns, Thomas S. Barbarians Within the Gates of Rome : A Study of Roman Military Policy and the Barbarians, ca. 375–425 A. D. Indiana University Press 1994. ISBN 978-0-253-31288-4.

Börm, Henning. Westrom. Von Honorius bis Justinian. Kohlhammer Verlag 2013. ISBN 978-3-17-023276-1 (Review in English).

Cameron, Alan (2010). The Last Pagans of Rome. Oxford University Press. ISBN 978-0-19-974727-6.

Cameron, Averil. The Mediterranean World in Late Antiquity. AD 395–700. Routledge 2011, ISBN 978-0415579612.

Connolly, Peter. Greece and Rome at War. Revised edition, Greenhill Books, 1998. ISBN 978-1-85367-303-0.

Errington, R. Malcolm (2006). Roman Imperial Policy from Julian to Theodosius. Chapel Hill: University of North Carolina Press. ISBN 0-8078-3038-0.

Gaddis, Michael. There Is No Crime for Those Who

Have Christ. Religious violence in the Christian Roman Empire. University of California Press, 2005. ISBN 978-0-520-24104-6.

Galinsky, Karl. Classical and Modern Interactions (1992) 53–73.

Gibbon, Edward. History of the Decline and Fall of the Roman Empire. With notes by the Rev. H. H. Milman. 1782 (Written), 1845 (Revised)

Goldsworthy, Adrian. The complete Roman Army. ISBN 978-0-500-05124-5. Thames & Hudson, 2003.

Goldsworthy, Adrian. The Fall of the West: The Slow Death of the Roman Superpower. ISBN 978-0-7538-2692-8. Phoenix, an imprint of Orion Books Ltd, 2010.

Graf, Fritz (2014). "Laying Down the Law in Ferragosto: The Roman Visit of Theodosius in Summer 389". Journal of Early Christian Studies. 22 (2): 219–242. doi:10.1353/earl.2014.0022. S2CID 159641057.

Heather, Peter. The fall of the Roman Empire. A new history. Pan Books, 2006. ISBN 978-0-330-49136-5.

Halsall, Guy. Barbarian Migrations and the Roman West, 376–568 (Cambridge Medieval Textbooks)

Harper, Kyle. The fate of Rome. Climate, disease, and the end of an empire. ISBN 978-0-691-19206-2. Princeton University Press 2017.

Harper, Kyle. Slavery in the late Roman world AD 275–425. ISBN 978-0-521-19861-5. Cambridge University Press 2011.

Hunt, Lynn, Thomas R. Martin, Barbara H. Rosenwein, R. Po-chia Hsia, Bonnie G. Smith. The Making of the West, Peoples and Cultures, Volume A: To 1500. Bedford / St. Martins 2001. ISBN 0-312-18365-8.

Hodges, Richard, Whitehouse, David. Mohammed, Charlemagne and the Origins of Europe: archaeology and the Pirenne thesis. Cornell University Press, 1983.

Jones, A. H. M. The Later Roman Empire, 284–602: A Social, Economic, and Administrative Survey [Paperback, vol. 1] ISBN 0-8018-3353-1 Basil Blackwell Ltd. 1964.

Lavan, Luke & Michael Mulryan, eds. (2011). The Archaeology of Late Antique 'Paganism'. Leiden: Brill. ISBN 978-90-04-19237-9.

Letki Piotr. The cavalry of Diocletian. Origin, organization, tactics, and weapons. Translated by Pawel Grysztar and Trystan Skupniewicz. Wydawnictwo NapoleonV ISBN 978-83-61324-93-5. Oświęcim 2012.

Macgeorge, Penny. Late Roman Warlords. Oxford University Press 2002.

MacMullen, Ramsay. Corruption and the decline of Rome. Yale University Press, 1988. ISBN 0-300-04799-1.

Martindale, J.R. The Prosopography of the Later Roman Empire volume II, A.D. 395–527. Cambridge University Press 1980.

Matthews, John. The Roman empire of Ammianus. Michigan Classical Press, 2007. ISBN 978-0-9799713-2-7.

Matthews, John. Western aristocracies and Imperial court AD 364–425. Oxford University Press 1975. ISBN 0-19-814817-8.

Momigliano, Arnaldo. 1973. "La caduta senza rumore di un impero nel 476 d.C." ("The noiseless fall of an empire in 476 AD"). Rivista storica italiana, 85 (1973),

5–21.

Nicasie, M. J. Twilight of Empire. The Roman Army from the reign of Diocletian to the Battle of Adrianople. J. C. Gieben, 1998. ISBN 90-5063-448-6.

Randsborg, Klavs. The First Millennium AD in Europe and the Mediterranean: an archaeological essay. Cambridge University Press 1991. ISBN 0 521 38401 X.

Rathbone, Dominic. "Earnings and Costs. Part IV, chapter 15", pp. 299–326. In: Quantifying the Roman Economy. Methods and Problems. Alan Bowman and Andrew Wilson eds. Oxford University Press 2009, paperback edition 2013, ISBN 978-0-19-967929-4.

Ward-Perkins Bryan. The fall of Rome and the end of civilization. Oxford University Press 2005 (hardback edition). ISBN 978-0-19-280728-1

Woods, David. "Theodosius I (379–395 A.D.)". De Imperatoribus Romanis.

## Further Reading about the Fall of Constantinople

Ball, Warwick (2016). Rome in the East: Transformation of an Empire, 2nd edition. London & New York: Routledge, ISBN 978-0-415-72078-6.

Bury, J. B. (1958). History of the Later Roman Empire: From the Death of Theodosius I to the Death of Justinian. Dover Publications.

Crowley, Roger (2005). Constantinople: Their Last Great Siege, 1453. Faber and Faber. ISBN 978-0-571-22185-1.

Freely, John (1998). Istanbul: The Imperial City. Penguin. ISBN 978-0-14-024461-8.

Freely, John; Ahmet S. Cakmak (2004). The Byzantine Monuments of Istanbul. Cambridge University Press. ISBN 978-0-521-77257-0.

Gibbon, Edward (2005). The Decline and Fall of the Roman Empire. Phoenix Press. ISBN 978-0-7538-1881-7.

Hanna-Riitta, Toivanen (2007). The Influence of Constantinople on Middle Byzantine Architecture (843–1204). A typological and morphological approach at the provincial level. Suomen kirkkohistoriallisen seuran toimituksia 202 (Publications of the Finnish Society of Church History No. 202). ISBN 978-952-5031-41-6.

Harris, Jonathan. Constantinople: Capital of Byzantium. Bloomsbury, 2nd edition, 2017. ISBN 978-1-4742-5465-6.

Harris, Jonathan. Byzantium and the Crusades. Bloomsbury, 2nd edition, 2014. ISBN 978-1-78093-767-0.

Herrin, Judith (2008). Byzantium: The Surprising Life of a Medieval Empire. Princeton University Press. ISBN 978-0-691-13151-1.

Hirth, Friedrich (2000) [1885]. Jerome S. Arkenberg, ed. "East Asian History Sourcebook: Chinese Accounts of Rome, Byzantium and the Middle East, c. 91 B.C.E. – 1643 C.E." Fordham.edu. Fordham University. Retrieved 2016-09-10.

Janin, Raymond (1964). Constantinople Byzantine (in French) (2 ed.). Paris: Institut Français d'Etudes Byzantines.

Korolija Fontana-Giusti, Gordana 'The Urban Language of Early Constantinople: The Changing Roles of the Arts and Architecture in the Formation of the New Capital and the New Consciousness' in Intercultural Transmission in the Medieval Mediterranean, (2012), Stephanie L. Hathaway and David W. Kim (eds), London: Continuum, pp 164–202. ISBN 978-1-4411-3908-5.

Mamboury, Ernest (1953). The Tourists' Istanbul. Istanbul: Çituri Biraderler Basımevi.

Mansel, Philip (1998). Constantinople: City of the World's Desire, 1453–1924. St. Martin's Griffin. ISBN 978-0-312-18708-8.

Meyendorff, John (1996). Rome, Constantinople, Moscow: Historical and Theological Studies. Crestwood, NY: St. Vladimir's Seminary Press. ISBN 9780881411348.

Müller-Wiener, Wolfgang (1977). Bildlexikon zur Topographie Istanbuls: Byzantion, Konstantinupolis, Istanbul bis zum Beginn d. 17 Jh (in German). Tübingen: Wasmuth. ISBN 978-3-8030-1022-3.

Phillips, Jonathan (2005). The Fourth Crusade and the Sack of Constantinople. Pimlico. ISBN 978-1-84413-080-1.

Runciman, Steven (1990). The Fall of Constantinople, 1453. Cambridge University Press. ISBN 978-1-84413-080-1.

Treadgold, Warren (1997). A History of the Byzantine State and Society. Stanford University Press. ISBN 978-0-8047-2630-6.

Yule, Henry (1915). Henri Cordier (ed.), Cathay and the Way Thither: Being a Collection of Medieval Notices of China, Vol I: Preliminary Essay on the Intercourse Between China and the Western Nations Previous to the Discovery of the Cape Route. London: Hakluyt Society. Accessed 21 September 2016.

Evans, Helen C.; Wixom, William D (1997). The glory of Byzantium: art and culture of the Middle Byzantine era, A.D. 843–1261. New York: The Metropolitan Museum of Art. ISBN 978-0-8109-6507-2. Retrieved 2016-02-19.

Bogdanović, Jelena (2016). The Relational Spiritual Geopolitics of Constantinople, the Capital of the

Byzantine Empire. Boulder : University Press of Colorado.

Printed in Great Britain
by Amazon